W9-DFD-874

Going Beyond Vaikuṇṭha

Gaudiya Vedanta Outreach
347 7278692
Vasantidasi@gmail.com
www.gvoutreach.com

BOOKS BY
ŚRĪ ŚRĪMAD BHAKTIVEDĀNTA NĀRĀYAṆA GOSVĀMĪ MAHĀRĀJA

Arcana-dīpikā
Beyond Nīrvāṇa
Śrī Bhajana-rahasya
Śrī Bhakti-rasāmṛta-sindhu-bindu
Bhakti-rasāyana
Bhakti-tattva-viveka
Śrī Brahma-saṁhitā
Essence of the Bhagavad-gītā
Five Essential Essays
Harmony
Jaiva-dharma
Letters From America
Śrī Manaḥ-śikṣā
My Śikṣā-guru and Priya-bandhu
Pinnacle of Devotion
Śrī Prabandhāvalī
Secret Truths of the Bhagavatam
Secrets of the Undiscovered Self
Śiva-tattva
Śrī Bṛhad-bhāgavatāmṛta
Śrī Camatkāra-candrikā
Śrī Dāmodarāṣṭakam
Śrī Gauḍīya Gīti-guccha
Śrī Gītā-govinda
Śrī Gopi-gīta
Śrī Harināma Mahā-mantra
Śrī Navadvīpa-dhāma-māhātmya
Śrī Navadvīpa-dhāma Parikramā
Śrī Prema-sampuṭa
Śrī Rādhā-kṛṣṇa-gaṇoddeśa-dīpikā
Śrī Saṅkalpa-kalpadrumaḥ
Śrī Śikṣāṣṭaka
Śrī Upadeśāmṛta
Śrī Vraja-maṇḍala Parikramā
Śrī Rāya Rāmānanda Saṁvāda
Śrīla Bhakti Prajñāna Keśava Gosvāmī – His Life and Teachings
The Distinctive Contribution of Śrīla Rūpa Gosvāmī
The Essence of All Advice
The Gift of Śrī Caitanya Mahāprabhu
The Journey of the Soul
The Nectar of Govinda-līlā
The Origin of Ratha-yātrā
The Way of Love
Utkalikā-vallarī
Vaiṣṇava-siddhānta-mālā
Veṇu-gīta
Walking with a Saint
Rays of the Harmonist (periodical)

For further information, free downloads of all titles, world tour lectures, and more, please visit our websites:

www.purebhakti.com
www.purebhakti.tv
www.backtobhakti.com
www.bhaktistore.com

śrī śrī guru-gaurāṅgau jayataḥ

Going Beyond Vaikuṇṭha

ŚRĪ ŚRĪMAD
BHAKTIVEDĀNTA NĀRĀYAṆA
GOSVĀMĪ MAHĀRĀJA

VṚNDĀVANA • NEW DELHI • SAN FRANCISCO

© 1994 GAUDIYA VEDANTA PUBLICATIONS. SOME RIGHTS RESERVED.

EXCEPT WHERE OTHERWISE NOTED, CONTENT IN THIS BOOK IS LICENSED UNDER THE CREATIVE COMMONS ATTRIBUTION-NO DERIVATIVE WORKS 3.0 UNPORTED LICENSE.

To view a copy of this license, visit http://creativecommons.org/licenses/by-nd/3.0/
Permissions beyond the scope of this license may be available at
www.purebhakti.com/pluslicense or write to: gvp.contactus@gmail.com

Artwork on the front cover by Śyāmarāṇī dāsī
© The Bhaktivedanta Book Trust. Used with permission.
Photograph of Śrīla Bhaktivedānta Svāmī Mahārāja © The Bhaktivedanta Book Trust.
Used with permission. All rights reserved. www.krishna.com
Photograph of Śrīla Bhaktivedānta Nārāyaṇa Gosvāmī Mahārāja
© Subala-sakhā dāsa. Used with permission.
We are grateful to those who financially contributed to this edition, especially
Jagannātha dāsa and Kṛṣṇa-līlā dāsī (Fiji) www.mygvp.com

Going Beyond Vaikuṇṭha, 4th edition

First edition:	June 1994 – 1,000 copies
Second edition:	September 1997 – 2,000 copies
Third edition:	September 2006 – 1,000 copies
Fourth edition:	September 2011 – 2,000 copies
	December 2013 – 2,000 copies

Printed at Spectrum Printing Press Pvt. Ltd.,
New Delhi (India)

ISBN 978-1-935428-40-4

Library of Congress Control Number 2011937005

British Library Cataloging in Publication Data. A catalogue record for this book is available from the British Library

Cataloging in Publication Data--DK
Courtesy: D.K. Agencies (P) Ltd. <docinfo@dkagencies.com>

Bhaktivedānta Nārāyaṇa, 1921-
Going beyond Vaikuṇṭha / Bhaktivedānta Nārāyaṇa Gosvāmī Mahārāja. -- 4th ed.
p. cm.
Includes verses in Sanskrit (roman).
Translated from Hindi.
Includes index.
ISBN 9781935428404

1. Sanātana Goswāmī, 1484-1558. Bhāgavatāmṛta.
2. Krishna (Hindu deity) in literature. I. Title.

DDC 891.21 23

Contents

Chapter

Publisher's Note

The Path of Love

The soul's nature is to seek real freedom, to hanker for lasting pleasure. We seek satisfaction and happiness in the world around us, but our experiences over time expose the futility of such ephemeral pleasure. Enlightened souls, who are full of compassion, describe the reality of a permanent bliss based on a lasting spiritual existence. Their writings provide us with an intimate insight into reality, which is replete with variety, form, qualities and exquisite, lustrous personalities. Their writings also invite us to participate in the sweetness of ever-increasing transcendental love, or *prema*. They thus direct us to that ultimate destination, which is achieved by attaining the spiritual perfection that they themselves possess. What they describe is called the path of love, distinct among the philosophies of India as *bhakti-yoga*, or devotion to God.

The Great Master

Bhakti-yoga is the essence of the Vedas (India's vast body of ancient Sanskrit scriptures; *veda* means "knowledge"). It is the path that all paths ultimately lead to, since it reveals the topmost condition of the heart. Although *bhakti-yoga* has been practised since time immemorial, the *bhakti-yoga* movement underwent a renaissance five hundred years ago in Bengal, coinciding with Europe's own Renaissance period.

The leading figure and reformer of this *bhakti* movement was Śrī Kṛṣṇa Caitanya, also known as Mahāprabhu, 'the Great Master'. The general populace of India regard Śrī Caitanya Mahāprabhu as a most extraordinary saint, but actually, He is an *avatāra*, an incarnation of the Lord who comes to this world with a specific mission.

He chose to incarnate as compassion personified in order to benefit the world in the troubled Age of Kali (our current epoch, the age of quarrel and hypocrisy).

According to Śrī Caitanya Mahāprabhu, worldly social distinctions are utterly irrelevant to one's eternal spiritual identity, which can easily be realized by chanting the names of God in the *mahā-mantra* – Hare Kṛṣṇa, Hare Kṛṣṇa, Kṛṣṇa Kṛṣṇa, Hare Hare, Hare Rāma, Hare Rāma, Rāma Rāma, Hare Hare.

The Mahā-mantra

The Hare Kṛṣṇa *mahā-mantra* is Śrī Rādhā and Śrī Kṛṣṇa personified as sacred sound. The vibration of the *mantra* is not a material sound as it comes directly from the spiritual platform and is beyond the realm of the mind. One can chant it all day and night and never feel tired. The more one chants, the more our spiritual consciousness is revived. The *mahā-mantra* consists of three words: Hare, Kṛṣṇa, and Rāma. Each word is in the vocative, a calling out to Rādhā and Kṛṣṇa.

Kṛṣṇa is the source of all spiritual potency and Śrī Rādhā is the complete embodiment of that potency. She is known as Hara (one who steals away) because She can captivate Kṛṣṇa's mind. In the vocative case, "Hara" becomes "Hare". Because He bestows bliss upon the residents of Vṛndāvana, He is referred to as Kṛṣṇa, the all-attractive one. The extraordinary beauty of His transcendental form always surcharges the minds and senses of the cowherd damsels and the other residents of Vraja with ever increasing spiritual bliss. For this reason He is glorified as Rāma.

The Supreme Form of Godhead

Śrī Kṛṣṇa (God) has many forms. All of them are perfect, but the Vedic scriptures state that Śrī Kṛṣṇa's original form in Vṛndāvana is the 'most perfect'. That holy abode is fully resplendent with His sweetness, which even predominates over His divine opulence. The residents of that holy place are imbued with such elevated feelings for the Supreme Lord that their worship of Him is devoid of the reverence normally offered to God. Those with a parental relationship with Him chastise Him, His friends defeat Him in games and order Him about, and His beloved *gopīs* sometimes become angry with Him and refuse to speak with Him. Such familiar and charming exchanges please Him unlimitedly more than exalted, reverential prayers offered by persons who do not have the same purity of love for Him.

In his preface to *Kṛṣṇa, The Supreme Personality of Godhead,* Śrīla Bhaktivedānta Svāmī Mahārāja states, "Kṛṣṇa is all-attractive, one should know that all his desires should be focused on Kṛṣṇa. In the *Bhagavad-gītā* it is said that the individual person is the proprietor or master of his own body but that Kṛṣṇa, who is the Supersoul present in everyone's heart, is the supreme proprietor and supreme master of each and every individual body. As such, if we concentrate our loving propensities upon Kṛṣṇa only, then immediately universal love, unity and tranquillity will be automatically realized. When one waters the root of a tree, he automatically waters the branches, twigs, leaves and flowers; when one supplies food to the stomach through the mouth, he satisfies all the various parts of the body."

This book, which reveals wonderful truths about the Supreme Person, will satisfy any sincere seeker of the Truth.

About the Author

On the auspicious day of Maunī Amāvasyā, 1921, Śrī Śrīmad Bhaktivedānta Nārāyaṇa Gosvāmī Mahārāja took his divine birth in a devout Vaiṣṇava family in Tivārīpura, in the state of Bihar, India.

In February, 1946, he met his *gurudeva*, Śrī Śrīmad Bhakti Prajñāna Keśava Gosvāmī Mahārāja, and his life of complete and exemplary dedication to Gauḍīya Vaiṣṇavism, or the path of *kṛṣṇa-bhakti* in the line of Śrī Caitanya Mahāprabhu, began.

He accompanied his *gurudeva* on his extensive preaching tours throughout India, actively assisting him in propagating the teachings of Śrī Caitanya Mahāprabhu for the eternal benefit of the living entities in this world. This included regularly hosting the thousands of pilgrims attending the yearly circumambulation of Śrī Navadvīpa-dhāma, the appearance place of Śrī Caitanya Mahāprabhu and Śrī Vṛndāvana-dhāma, the appearance place of Śrī Kṛṣṇa.

His *gurudeva* had instructed him to translate the writings of prominent Gauḍīya Vaiṣṇavas into Hindi, a task he assiduously assumed throughout his entire life and which resulted in the publication of nearly fifty Hindi sacred texts. These invaluable masterpieces are currently being translated into English and other major languages of the world.

For many years, he travelled throughout India to spread the message of Gauḍīya Vaiṣṇavism, and it was for this end, also, that in 1996, he journeyed abroad. During the next fourteen years, he circled the globe more than thirty times. Whether he was in India or abroad, his preaching always bore the distinctive characteristic of boldly unmasking any misconception obscuring the specific purposes of Śrī Caitanya Mahāprabhu's advent, in strict adherence to the desire of Śrīla Bhaktisiddhānta Sarasvatī Ṭhākura Prabhupāda and in perfect congruence with the conceptions of Śrīla Rūpa Gosvāmī, Śrī Caitanya Mahāprabhu's foremost follower. Thus, in present times, in upholding the glorious tenets of the Gauḍīya *sampradāya*, he performed the function of a true *ācārya*.

❋❋❋❋❋

At the age of ninety years, on December 29, 2010, at Cakra-tīrtha in Śrī Jagannātha Purī-dhāma, he concluded his pastimes in this world. The following day, in Śrī Navadvīpa-dhāma, Śrī Gaurasundara's fully empowered emissary, the very embodiment of His unique compassion, was given *samādhi*. He will never cease to reside in his divine instructions and in the hearts of those who are devoted to him.

nitya-līlā-praviṣṭa oṁ viṣṇupāda

Śrī Śrīmad Bhaktivedānta Nārāyaṇa Gosvāmī Mahārāja

nitya-līlā-praviṣṭa oṁ viṣṇupāda
ŚRĪ ŚRĪMAD BHAKTIVEDĀNTA VĀMANA GOSVĀMĪ MAHĀRĀJA

nitya-līlā-praviṣṭa oṁ viṣṇupāda
ŚRĪ ŚRĪMAD BHAKTIVEDĀNTA SVĀMĪ MAHĀRĀJA

nitya-līlā-praviṣṭa oṁ viṣṇupāda
ŚRĪ ŚRĪMAD BHAKTI PRAJÑĀNA KEŚAVA GOSVĀMĪ MAHĀRĀJA

nitya-līlā-praviṣṭa oṁ viṣṇupāda
ŚRĪ ŚRĪMAD BHAKTISIDDHĀNTA SARASVATĪ PRABHUPĀDA

Painting used with permission © Gaurahari dāsa

By relating the story of Gopa-kumāra, Parīkṣit Mahārāja explained to his mother in a very simple and charming way how we can attain *prema*, love of God. (Page 4)

Painting by Śyāmarāṇī dāsī © The Bhaktivedanta Book Trust. Used with permission.

We must accept *dīkṣā*, or initiation, offer intimate service to the *guru*, and accept instruction from him. We must simply serve the *guru* and Vaiṣṇavas, and keep arrogance far away by cultivating humility and not thinking highly of ourselves. (Page 4)

Painting used with permission © Hari-priya dāsī

Kāmākhyā-devī, upon seeing a person's nature, will act accordingly. Seeing that this *brāhmaṇa* was a resident of Govardhana, she decided that he should not be cheated in any way. Understanding his simple nature, she gave him the *gopāla-mantra.* (Page 9)

Painting used with permission © Gaurahari dāsa

The *brāhmaṇa* said, "I have come from afar, and in my heart there is a strong desire to know one thing: what is *sādhyā*, the final goal, and *sādhana*, the method to attain it?" (Page 14)

Painting used with permission © Sarasvatī dāsī

Śrī Kṛṣṇa was suddenly present before him. Gopa-kumāra cried out, "Oh! My very life!" and raced after Him. Coming near Kṛṣṇa, he tried to embrace Him, but just then Kṛṣṇa disappeared. Crying and crying in deep separation, Gopa-kumāra fell to the ground unconscious. While in his unconscious state, he saw a beautiful golden airplane appear before him at the speed of mind. (Page 29)

Painting used with permission © Bakulā dāsī

When you go before Him [Śrī Nārāyaṇa], He lifts His right hand in bestowal of blessings: "May all auspiciousness be upon you.... You will be fearless. All good fortune shall attend you." You want to race to embrace Him, and you want to play the flute with Him, but you are not able to do any of this. (Page 46–47)

Introduction

This book is a collection of lectures delivered by one of the most renowned Vaiṣṇava preceptors of modern times, our beloved *gurudeva, oṁ viṣṇupāda aṣṭottara-śata* Śrī Śrīmad Bhaktivedānta Nārāyaṇa Mahārāja. Spoken originally in Hindi, these lectures were recorded in January 1991 at Śrī Keśavajī Gauḍīya Maṭha in Mathurā,Uttar Pradesh, India. They comprise a single instalment of an immaculate running commentary that Śrīla Gurudeva spoke over a period of two years on Śrīla Sanātana Gosvāmīpāda's *Bṛhad-bhāgavatāmṛta*. Each chapter of this book is comprised of a single lecture, totalling twelve in all. The *Bṛhad-bhāgavatāmṛta* is a lengthy scripture, and the material included here covers exclusively verses from the fourth chapter of the second part.

Described herein is how, although having recently arrived in Śrī Vaikuṇṭha-dhāma, the most desirable of places and the entrance to which is sought after by unlimited saintly persons, Gopa-kumāra is feeling despondent and cannot even ascertain the cause of his own dissatisfaction. At that time he is approached by Śrī Nārada Ṛṣi, who becomes his instructing spiritual master and enlightens him with the understanding necessary to complete his spiritual journey and thereby attain the fulfilment of all his long-cherished internal desires. Gopa-kumāra's consequent determination to attain the eternal company of Śrī Kṛṣṇa in Vraja inspires him to continue chanting his *gopāla-mantra* until he is fully successful. Devotees who themselves sincerely yearn to one day go beyond Vaikuṇṭha and enter Śrī Goloka-Vraja, the transcendental land of spontaneous loving devotion to Śrī Śrī Rādhā-Govinda, will find the story of Gopa-kumāra particularly useful.

In his ongoing publication of Vaiṣṇava literature in the English language, Śrīla Gurudeva mentions repeatedly that he is simply following in the footsteps of his dear friend and instructing spiritual master, *nitya-līlā-praviṣṭa oṁ viṣṇupāda* Śrī Śrīmad A.C. Bhaktivedānta Swami Prabhupāda. Śrīla Prabhupāda singlehandedly and in a relatively short period of time spread the teachings of Kṛṣṇa consciousness around the entire world. His translations and writings set the standard for the literary presentation of Vaiṣṇava philosophy, and we sincerely pray that our current efforts are pleasing to him.

Grateful acknowledgement is extended to Lavaṅga-latā dāsī for copy-editing this new third edition, to Śānti dāsī for proofreading the final manuscript, to Atula-kṛṣṇa dāsa and Ananta-kṛṣṇa dāsa for checking the Sanskrit, to Kṛṣṇa-prema dāsa for designing the new cover and to Subala-sakhā dāsa for providing the new photograph of Śrīla Nārāyaṇa Mahārāja. Together we offer it into the hands of Śrīla Gurudeva, the crown jewel of *rasika* Vaiṣṇavas, praying that he will bless us with the necessary qualification to continue serving him in this capacity.

An aspiring servant of the Vaiṣṇavas

Prema-vilāsa dāsa

Pāpāṅkuśa-ekādaśī
5th October, 2003
Gopīnātha-bhavana, Śrī Vṛndāvana

Maṅgalācaraṇa

oṁ ajñāna-timirāndhasya
jñānāñjana-śalākayā
cakṣur unmīlitaṁ yena
tasmai śri-gurave namaḥ

I offer my most humble prostrated obeisances unto the spiritual master, who has opened my eyes, which were blinded by the darkness of ignorance, with the torchlight of knowledge.

vāñchā-kalpa-tarubhyaś ca
kṛpā-sindhubhya eva ca
patitānāṁ pāvenebhyo
vaiṣṇavebhyo namo namaḥ

I offer obeisances to the Vaiṣṇavas, who just like desire trees can fulfil the desires of everyone and who are full of compassion for conditioned souls.

namo mahā-vadānyāya
kṛṣṇa-prema-pradāya te
kṛṣṇāya kṛṣṇa-caitanya
nāmne gaura-tviṣe namaḥ

I offer obeisances to Śrī Caitanya Mahāprabhu, who is Kṛṣṇa Himself. He has assumed the golden hue of Śrīmatī Rādhikā and is munificently distributing *kṛṣṇa-prema.*

he kṛṣṇa karuṇā-sindho
dīna-bandho jagat-pate
gopeśa gopikā-kānta
rādhā-kānta namo 'stu te

I offer obeisances to Śrī Kṛṣṇa, who is an ocean of mercy, the friend of the distressed and the source of all creation. He is the master of the *gopas* and the lover of the *gopīs* headed by Śrīmatī Rādhikā.

tapta-kāñcana-gaurāṅgi
rādhe vṛndāvaneśvari
vṛṣabhānu-sute devi
praṇamāmi hari-priye

I offer obeisances to Śrīmatī Rādhikā, whose complexion is like molten gold and who is the queen of Vṛndāvana. She is the daughter of Vṛṣabhānu Mahārāja and is very dear to Śrī Kṛṣṇa.

hā devi kāku-bhara-gadgadayādya vācā
yāce nipatya bhuvi daṇḍavad udbhaṭārtiḥ
asya prasādam abudhasya janasya kṛtvā
gāndharvike nija gane gaṇanāṁ vidhehi

O Devī Gāndharvikā, in utter desperation I throw myself on the ground like a stick and with a choked voice humbly implore You to please be merciful to this fool and count me as one of Your own.

aṅga-śyāmalima-cchaṭābhir abhito mandīkṛtendīvaraṁ
jāḍyaṁ jāguḍa-rociṣāṁ vidadhataṁ paṭṭāmbarasya śriyā
vṛndāraṇya-nivāsinaṁ hṛdi lasad-dāmābhir āmodaraṁ
rādhā-skandha-niveśitojjvala-bhujaṁ dhyāyema dāmodaram

Whose dark bodily lustre is millions of times more beautiful than the blue lotus flower, whose efulgent yellow garments rebuke the radiance of golden *kuṅkuma*, whose residence is Śrī Vṛndāvana-*dhāma*, whose chest is beautified by a swinging *vaijayantī* garland, and whose splendorous left hand rests upon the right shoulder of Śrīmatī Rādhikā – I meditate upon that Śrī Dāmodara.

bhaktyā vihīnā aparādha-lakṣyaiḥ
kṣiptāś ca kāmādi-taraṅga-madhye
kṛpā-mayi tvāṁ śaraṇaṁ prapannā
vṛnde numaste caraṇāravindam

Devoid of devotion and guilty of committing unlimited offences, I am being tossed about in the ocean of material existence by the turbulent waves of lust, anger, greed and so forth. Therefore, O merciful Vṛndā-devī, I take shelter of you and offer obeisances unto your lotus feet.

gurave gauracandrāya
rādhikāyai tad-ālaye
kṛṣṇāya kṛṣṇa-bhaktāya
tad-bhaktāya namo namaḥ

I offer obeisances to the spiritual master, to Śrī Gauracandra, to Śrīmatī Rādhikā and Her associates, to Śrī Kṛṣṇa and His devotees, and to all Vaiṣṇavas.

vairāgya-yug-bhakti-rasaṁ prayatnair
apāyayan mām anabhīpsum andham
kṛpāmbhudhir yaḥ para-duḥkha-duḥkhī
sanātanaṁ taṁ prabhum āśrayāmi

I was unwilling to drink the nectar of *bhakti* possessed of renunciation, but Śrī Sanātana Gosvāmī, being an ocean of mercy who cannot tolerate the sufferings of others, made me drink it. Therefore I take shelter of him as my master.

śrī-caitanya-mano-'bhīṣṭaṁ
sthāpitaṁ yena bhūtale
svayaṁ rūpaḥ kadā mahyaṁ
dadāti sva-padāntikam

When will Śrī Rūpa Gosvāmī, who has established the mission in this world that fulfils the internal desire of Śrī Caitanya Mahāprabhu, give me shelter at his lotus feet?

yaṁ pravrajantam anupetam apeta-kṛtyaṁ
dvaipāyano viraha-kātara ājuhāva
putreti tan-mayatayā taravo 'bhinedus
taṁ sarva-bhūta-hṛdayaṁ munim ānato 'smi

I offer obeisances to Śrī Śukadeva Gosvāmī, who can enter the hearts of all living entities. When he left home without undergoing the purificatory processes such as accepting the sacred thread, his father Vyāsa cried out, "Oh my son!" As if they were absorbed in that same feeling of separation, only the trees echoed in response to his call.

tavaivāsmi tavaivāsmi
na jīvāmi tvayā vinā
iti vijñāya devi tvaṁ
naya māṁ caraṇāntikam

I am Yours! I am Yours! I cannot live without You! O Devī (Rādhā), please understand this and bring me to Your feet.

Chapter One

The Brāhmaṇa Meets Gopa-kumāra

The *Śrī Bṛhad-bhāgavatāmṛta* contains many fine topics concerning *bhakti*. By hearing them with great attention and interest, certainly a sublime type of 'greed' will arise, and that greed will move us in the direction of Vraja. For any *sādhaka* who desires spontaneous devotion (*rāgānuga-bhakti*), *Bṛhad-bhāgavatāmṛta* is very useful. How we can enter into devotion unto the Supreme Lord Śrī Kṛṣṇa (*bhagavad-bhakti*) and what is the nature of that devotion – this book describes both of these topics completely.

After *Śrīmad-Bhāgavatam* was spoken in seven days, the mother of Parīkṣit Mahārāja, Uttarā, said to her son, "Because what Śukadeva Gosvāmī explained was so philosophical and full of *siddhānta*, I was not able to experience it in my heart due to being a woman. Therefore please explain the essence of it in a simple fashion, in a few words only, so that I may understand it well."

Then Parīkṣit Mahārāja described how Nārada, from his own experience, showed the glories of Bhagavān by revealing the glories of His *dhāma* and the glories of His eternal associates. Nārada, by going to different holy places and different worlds, achieved knowledge of Bhagavān (*bhagavat-tattva*), and he experienced how Bhagavān is one yet expands into many. Similarly, the *dhāma* is one, with Vṛndāvana as the original *dhāma*, and it expands into many. And the original associates of Bhagavān are those of Vṛndāvana, and likewise they expand into many other worlds. This is the *siddhānta*: the one is expanded into many. Bhagavān is not two, three, ten or twenty. Nārada is the crown jewel of those who know this established truth (*tattva*), and he is *rasika*, expert in relishing *rasa*. So pretending that he didn't know any of this, Nārada began his journey.

First he met a *brāhmaṇa* worshipping his *śālagrāma-śilā*. He said to the *brāhmaṇa*, "In this world, you are surely fortunate." Beginning from there, he ultimately arrived at Dvārakā, where he realised the *gopīs* to be the topmost devotees. The *gopīs* of Vṛndāvana are categorically higher than those great souls who are situated in all the other *rasas*, and even higher than the queens of Dvārakā. And amongst all the *gopīs*, Śrīmatī Rādhikā is the best:

ārādhanānāṁ sarveṣāṁ
viṣṇor ārādhanaṁ param
tasmāt parataraṁ devi
tadīyānāṁ samarcanam

Padma Purāṇa

[Mahādeva told Durgā-devī:] Of all varieties of worship, worship of Viṣṇu is the best. But even better than that is the worship of those devotees related to Him.

In this verse the word *tadīyānāṁ* means 'those who have a relationship with Bhagavān'. There are so many who are related to Him, but amongst them, Śrīmatī Rādhikā is the best. Hearing all of this, Nārada became overwhelmed with divine love (*prema*). Especially in the pastime of constructing Nava-vṛndāvana in Dvārakā, he was shown the glories of the *gopīs*. Seeing how Kṛṣṇa was overwhelmed by separation from the *gopīs*, Satyabhāmā, Rukmiṇī, Jāmbavatī and all others became astonished. Nārada was very pleased, but then he began to feel ashamed, thinking, "By coming here today and making Kṛṣṇa remember the *gopīs*, I have given Him some pain and made Him fall unconscious."

Kṛṣṇa said, "You may ask any boon from Me."

Nārada replied, "Ask for a boon? I have committed a great offence at Your feet! I have given You so much trouble and made You fall unconscious."

Kṛṣṇa said, "If you had not done this, then the glories of My eternal associates in Vraja would never have been broadcast. Therefore you are worthy of taking a boon from Me. Tell Me what you would like."

So Nārada said, "My Lord, I want to always remember Your pastimes with the *gopīs* in Vṛndāvana. Wherever these pastimes are being performed, I want to go to that place and take the dust on my head. I want to always sing the *kīrtana* of those pastimes, and if You would be so merciful, please give me the *prema* of the *gopīs*."

Kṛṣṇa said, "So it shall be. Going to the places of My pastimes in Vraja – especially Nandagrāma, Varṣāṇā, Govardhana, Yāvaṭa, Ṭera-kadamba, Uddhava-kyārī, Vaṁśīvaṭa and Rādhā-kuṇḍa – with great love you should offer obeisances (*praṇāma*) and pray for their mercy. Then you will easily obtain that rare *prema* which even Brahmā desires."

According to the gradation of His associates, there is gradation in Bhagavān. There are so many different types of devotees, different types of pastimes, and different types of *rasa*. For the four Kumāras, Kṛṣṇa appears as Brahmā, for Viśvaksena and the devotees in Vaikuṇṭha He is Nārāyaṇa, for Hanumān He appears as Lord Rāmacandra, and for Satyabhāmā, Rukmiṇī and Uddhava He is Dvārakādhīśa. To the *gopas* He is a friend, to those in *vātsalya-rasa* He is a son, and to the *gopīs* He is the dearest lover: all are one and the same Kṛṣṇa. How is it possible to comprehend all of this? Only by the mercy of Bhagavān and His devotees will we be able to fully understand this; without their mercy it is not possible.

By relating the story of Gopa-kumāra, Parīkṣit Mahārāja explained to his mother in a very simple and charming way how we can attain *prema*. If anyone desires *prema* but performs no hearing (*śravaṇa*) and chanting (*kīrtana*), or thinks that he will attain it merely by his own endeavour, he will never get it.Without service to the spiritual master (*guru*) and service to the Vaiṣṇavas, then even after thousands of births or even after reading thousands of scriptures, one will still not be able to attain *prema*. Only by following the prescribed *sādhana* is it possible. It has been said that if we neglect the regulations of the Śruti, Smṛti and *Nārada-pañcarātra*, we will not attain exclusive *bhakti*, but only become confused. Therefore we must follow the rules and regulations. What are they? We must accept initiation (*dīkṣā*), offer intimate service to the *guru*, and accept instruction from him. We must simply serve the spiritual master and the Vaiṣṇavas, and keep arrogance far away by cultivating humility and not thinking highly of ourselves:

tṛṇād api sunīcena
taror api sahiṣṇunā
amāninā mānadena
kīrtanīyah sadā hariḥ

Śrī Śikṣāṣṭaka (3)

One should chant the holy name in a humble state of mind, thinking oneself to be more insignificant than a piece of straw. One should be more tolerant than a tree, free from false pride and ready to offer all respect to others.

The more we can follow this, then by the mercy of Bhagavān, and by the mercy of the Vaiṣṇavas – which is the very essence of the mercy of Bhagavān – the sooner *bhakti* will appear in our hearts.

If Bhagavān bestows His mercy on someone, then that person will attain *bhakti*. He has that power. But why does He give His mercy to some persons and not to others? In this world most people don't engage in *bhagavad-bhajana*, and to them He will not give His mercy. Then very few people will get His mercy. Why is this so? Because He doesn't consider everyone to be equal. If mercy is shown to some and not to others, it appears that the fault of partiality is present. If a devotee makes distinctions in regard to whom he is merciful, then it seems that the fault of partiality has appeared in his devotion. To give much love to one person, less to another; to give much instruction to one and less to another; to tell deep things to one and only superficial things to another – in this behaviour it seems there is the fault of partiality.

But there are three types of Vaiṣṇava: *uttama* (topmost), *madhyama* (intermediate) and *kaniṣṭha* (neophyte). *Uttama* Vaiṣṇavas have almost all the good qualities of Bhagavān. They don't experience the sufferings of ordinary people. They are *ātmārāma* (self-satisfied) and *āptakāma* (devoid of mundane desires). Even if some allurement comes before them, they are never disturbed and are always fixed in internal worship. They will not show kindness to anyone either, and even if someone dies they may remain indifferent. They are transcendental to the body and fully self-realised.

The *kaniṣṭha* Vaiṣṇava does not have sufficient knowledge of *tattva*, and is therefore unable to give mercy. And there are four symptoms of a *madhyama* Vaiṣṇava:

īśvare tad-adhīneṣu
bāliśeṣu dviṣatsu ca
prema-maitrī-kṛpopekṣā
yaḥ karoti sa madhyamaḥ

Śrīmad-Bhāgavatam (11.2.46)

For Bhagavān he has *prema*, and towards Vaiṣṇavas he has three types of friendly relations. Towards an *uttama* Vaiṣṇava he has a service attitude, with those on an equal footing to himself he will establish friendship, and towards a *kaniṣṭha* Vaiṣṇava he is merciful. He is completely indifferent to envious people, and to those who are ignorant but have a little faith, in a general way he is merciful.

In a *madhyama-adhikārī* there are these four types of partiality, but in an *uttama-adhikārī* there is no such partiality. He has the same outlook towards everyone. He doesn't see the difference between a conditioned soul and a liberated soul; he sees that everyone is liberated. Therefore he has no duty. But it is the duty of the *madhyama* Vaiṣṇava to have this partiality. Therefore who will give the mercy by which *bhakti* will arise? The *madhyama* Vaiṣṇava, and especially those that are higher *madhyama* Vaiṣṇavas, will give this mercy. One who is entering the realm of an *uttama* Vaiṣṇava – who is not there yet, but is qualified to cross the upper limit of the *madhyama* stage – is especially kind and merciful. He wants to distribute to others the wealth that he has stored inside his own heart. When he distributes mercy, the fault of partiality cannot be attributed to him, because according to the *Bhāgavatam*, it is actually a symptom of this stage to be partial. If we acquire the association of such a Vaiṣṇava, then we should serve him with our life and soul:

śuśrūṣsyā bhajana-vijñam ananyam anya-
nindādi-śūnya-hṛdam īpsita-saṅga-labdhyā

Upadeśāmṛta (5)

We should serve a Vaiṣṇava who is advanced in *bhakti* and whose heart is free from the tendency to criticise others.

If we achieve the association of such a Vaiṣṇava, then it is necessary for us to offer our head bowed to him in surrender. If there is any cheating tendency in our service, he will know of it. Just like Bhagavān, he can see inside us and he knows well peoples' cheating ways. He may dispense punishment to us, but in that there will also be mercy. Or upon perceiving our cheating he may be indifferent towards us, so in a straightforward manner we should serve him.

There are also two types of mercy from Vaiṣṇavas. One is mercy acquired in previous lives and the other is mercy acquired in this life. The accumulated pious merit from perhaps millions of lifetimes may result in one's receiving mercy from Vaiṣṇavas who are *rasika*, merciful by nature and knowledgeable in *tattva*, thereby leading one to take initiation from a genuine spiritual master and make progress on the path of *bhajana*. This is called *prāktana-saṁskāra*: that which has been acquired in previous births. Having such previous acquisition, in some very rare cases there may even be no necessity of formally accepting a *guru*. For instance, Haridāsa Ṭhākura and so many of the associates of Caitanya Mahāprabhu were already fully developed in *bhakti* and for them there was no necessity of taking formal initiation, but still they accepted it just to set an example for common people.

There is also the case of Bhārata Mahārāja. In his first birth he had a *guru*, but in his second and third births he did not formally accept a *guru*, yet still, without effort he attained the elevated stage of *bhāva*. He didn't listen to his father or anyone who tried to dissuade him from the path of *bhakti*. This is *prāktana-saṁskāra*, having which one will easily acquire an elevated *guru*, attain the association of advanced devotees (*sādhu-saṅga*), and very quickly feel devotional sentiment arise within him. Maybe only one verse of a scripture will be recited to him, and from that only, he will understand everything. Those who have this previous merit will have some taste (*ruci*) for devotional life, and will knowingly accept initiation from a *rasika* Vaiṣṇava. Then intense greed for *bhakti* will arise in them, and they will make rapid progress in *bhajana*.

As for those who don't have this previous merit, by hearing about the pastimes of Kṛṣṇa from *Śrīmad-Bhāgavatam* and by associating with Vaiṣṇavas, greed for *bhakti* will gradually arise in them. Then they will accept a *guru*. But they may accept a spiritual master whose thought is not in the right line, and so they will have to leave him and approach a genuinely spiritual *guru* whose *siddhānta* is correct. Or they may accept a real *guru* in the first place, and when that *guru* leaves this world, what must they do? Accept an instructing spiritual master (*śikṣā-guru*), a *rasika* Vaiṣṇava who is full of spiritual greed. These are the two types of mercy from Vaiṣṇavas.

In *Śrī Bṛhad-bhāgavatāmṛta*, Gopa-kumāra explains all of these points to a *brāhmaṇa* from his own life experience. This *brāhmaṇa* was a resident of Mathurā who went to Pragjyotisapura in Assam. Just as we see these days in Gujarat there are scholars who wander here and there speaking from the scriptures to make their living, so this *brāhmaṇa's* aim was like that. He was thinking that there was a great deal of money in Assam, and that somehow or other he would be able to make a living there. So he went there, and when he didn't make any money, he worshipped the goddess Kāmākhyā-devī (Pārvatī-devī). She became very pleased with him, and understanding his internal sentiment, thought, "It appears that he has some spiritual merit (*sukṛti*) from previous lives. If I give him just a little help, he will be able to go far. But first his desire for money must be eliminated, and then he will be able to go forward." She appeared before the *brāhmaṇa* and said, "You desire wealth? There is nothing greater than the treasure that I will give you."

What is the greatest wealth? *Bhakti*. If anyone approaches a genuine *guru* – even if that person is just an ignorant boy or girl and not able to understand much *siddhānta* – still, such a *guru* will slowly give them love for the Supreme Lord. But an impure *guru* will say, "Worship Devī, worship Gaṇeśa, worship Śaṅkara, and being pleased with you, they will give you whatever you desire."

Kāmākhyā-devī, upon seeing a person's nature, will act accord ingly. Seeing that this *brāhmaṇa* was a resident of Govardhana, she decided that he should not be cheated in any way. Understanding his simple nature, she gave him the *gopāla-mantra*.

For entrance into the topmost devotional mellow of amorous love (*mādhurya-rasa*), this *mantra* is especially necessary. By the mercy of Sanātana Gosvāmī and other exalted Vaiṣṇavas, the *gopāla-mantra* is now prevalent in our *sampradāya*. Before the appearance of Caitanya Mahāprabhu this *mantra* was not made available to everyone. It was only given to those who were understood to have the special qualification of sufficient merit from previous lifetimes.

Devī gave this *brāhmaṇa* her direct audience (*darśana*) and bestowed this *mantra* upon him. Chanting the *mantra*, his devotion became firm. Chanting more and more, he eventually lost his desire for wealth, and felt that he already possessed the very root of all wealth. From Assam he went to the ocean at Gangasagara and bathed, and becoming indifferent to that place, he went to Gaya. Feeling indifferent there, he went to Varanasi, where he became a little attracted to the conception of liberation (*mukti*). There Pārvatī-devī again blessed him with her *darśana*, yet this time she was accompanied by her husband Śaṅkara, who said, "Beware! Don't stay here! Go away from here immediately!"

If they are especially merciful to someone, they will instruct him in this way. Otherwise, one would remain there, and shaving his head, would begin chanting the famous impersonalist aphorisms '*ahaṁ brahmāsmi*', '*tat-tvam asi*' and '*sarvam-khalv idam-brahma*', aspiring for impersonal liberation. But being merciful to this *brāhmaṇa*, Mahādeva and Pārvatī told him, "Run away from here quickly; you mustn't stay! *Mukti* is like a tigress that will devour you, and you will never emerge from its mouth! Run from here quickly and don't turn back! Go straight to Mathurā, bathe at Viśrāma-ghāṭa, and then proceed directly to Vṛndāvana."

On the way the *brāhmaṇa* spent some time in Prayaga where he saw a crowd of thousands of people. Seated around a fire performing a sacrifice were great renunciants with their hair tied high on their heads and ashes smeared on their bodies. Others were giving lectures and readings and loudly chanting, "*Jaya* Śrī Rāma! *Jaya* Śrī Rāma!" For the month of Māgha [January–February] all types of holy men (*sādhus*) go there to bathe. The hermitage of Bharadvāja Ṛṣi where Vālmīki spent some time is there, and there also Rāmacandra crossed the Gaṅgā. It is a very pure place; Caitanya Mahāprabhu instructed Rūpa Gosvāmī there as well.

Seeing all of this, the *brāhmaṇa* thought, "If I could be like this also, it would be very good." The people were giving great respect to all of the saints there. He took *darśana* of the Bindu-Mādhava deity, attended the *ārati* ceremony and heard lectures. When some devotees started performing a *kīrtana*, he said, "What are you shouting? And what is all of this you are speaking in your discourses?"

They said to him, "Brother, don't speak out so brashly like this; it will be an offence (*aparādha*). The great souls (*mahātmās*) are describing the glories of Bhagavān Śrī Viṣṇu in their discourses."

Again the *brāhmaṇa* felt indifferent and left there. Following the instructions of Śaṅkara, he eventually arrived at Mathurā and bathed at Viśrāma-ghāṭa. In Varanasi, Śaṅkara had told him, "If you continue chanting your *mantra-japa*, your favourite deity will give you *darśana*."

Who is the deity of the *gopāla-mantra*? Gopāla-Kṛṣṇa. And which Gopāla-Kṛṣṇa? It is according to the particular sentiment of the devotee. To some it is that Gopāla who takes the cows out to graze, to some it is baby Kṛṣṇa sitting in the lap of Yaśodā, and for those in *mādhurya-rasa* it is Kiśora-Gopāla. For this *brāhmaṇa*, it was Kṛṣṇa taking the cows out to graze, playing the flute and wandering in the forests of Vṛndāvana in the company of His cowherd friends.

If we do not receive the *darśana* of Kṛṣṇa in our meditation while we are chanting our *mantra-japa*, in the higher sense we can understand it all to be useless. "When will it be? When will it be?" – we should have this eagerness. We should chant with our hearts, and then we will see that this *mantra* will bestow His direct *darśana*. Otherwise birth after birth it will be fruitless. If we are mindless while chanting, or worried, or sometimes falling asleep, or sometimes becoming discouraged, we will not receive the full result of the *mantra*. When will we get the full result of the *mantra*? When we chant in precisely the way that the spiritual master has taught us, and as Pārvatī instructed this *brāhmaṇa*: chanting with our concentration focused, ridding our hearts of all desires for sense enjoyment, with humility, and with tears coming to our eyes in remembrance – this will bring Gopāla. We must chant with a steady mind and exclusive sentiment, and eventually the *mantra* will give us direct *darśana* of Śrī Kṛṣṇa Himself:

gurau goṣṭhe goṣṭhālayiṣu sujane bhūsura-gaṇe sva-mantre

Śrī Manaḥ-śikṣā (1)

We should chant with peace of mind, love and firm faith, and then the *mantra* will give us direct *darśana* of our deity, and also *darśana* of our spiritual master.

After bathing at Viśrāma-ghāṭa, the *brāhmaṇa* entered Śrī Vṛndāvana. Eventually he arrived at the banks of the Yamunā, and at that time there was no town or village there. From a secluded grove (*kuñja*) he heard a voice lamenting, but it was also very sweet. He could not discern if it was someone crying, if it was a *kīrtana*, or even whether it was a man or woman, but the sound was attracting him. Slowly he began searching after this voice until he came to a dense *kuñja* amongst the gardens of the Yamunā near Keśī-ghāṭa. Entering the *kuñja*, he saw a very effulgent and attractive youth. It was Gopa-kumāra, and he was chanting this *kīrtana* in a very sweet melody:

> *śrī-kṛṣṇa gopāla hare mukunda*
> *govinda he nanda-kiśora kṛṣṇa*
> *hā śrī-yaśodā-tanaya prasīda*
> *śrī-ballavī-jīvana rādhikeśa*
>
> *Bṛhad-bhāgavatāmṛta* (2.4.7)

In his *kīrtana* he was emphasising the line *hā śrī-yasodā-tanaya prasīda*. He was shedding tears and saliva was falling from his mouth. Whether he was conscious or unconscious, the *brāhmaṇa* couldn't tell. Bringing some water from the Yamunā, the *brāhmaṇa* cleaned Gopa-kumāra's mouth, and fanning him, gradually brought him to his external senses. After a little while Gopa-kumāra arose and said, "You have come from Assam, from Pragjyotisapura? There the goddess Devī gave you some *mantra*?" The *brāhmaṇa* did not reply. "She gave you the *gopāla-mantra*? From there, via Gangasagara and Gaya, you went to Varanasi, and there Śaṅkara and Pārvatī gave you some instruction? And via Prayaga you have come here?"

The more Gopa-kumāra said, the more the *brāhmaṇa* was astonished, and deep faith arose in him towards Gopa-*kumāra*. Thinking, "How did he know this?" the *brāhmaṇa* could only stand motionlessly and listen, stunned. He was deeply affected. When we have this kind of experience, the faith that it produces will stay with us for our entire life. When we are fortunate enough to meet such a *guru*, the effect will be lasting. But upon meeting a bogus *guru* we will get a different feeling. The so-called *guru* will say, "My friend, please take *harināma* initiation from me."

One may reply, "No, not now; perhaps I will take it tomorrow or the next day."

But if the so-called *guru* sees that, "This man is wealthy and has a nice house and nice possessions; through him we can get some work done. There is some litigation against us, and since he has a post with the government, he can clear it up for us," then he will say, "No, there is no need to wait. Take it now; otherwise your mind will become distracted. Just bring a flower garland."

And even if one does not want to bring a garland, the false *guru* will say, "All right then; for you there will be no restriction in regard to eating and drinking, such as being vegetarian and abstaining from wine. Whose *mantra* do you want? Would you like the Gaṇeśa *mantra*?"

A pure *guru* will not do any of this funny business with *mantras*. He will thoughtfully determine the sentiment of a prospective disciple, and if the person has a genuine desire for *kṛṣṇa-bhakti*, then he will give him the *mantra*. Otherwise, on some pretext he will postpone it and send the person away. Especially if a *madhyama-adhikārī* spiritual master is a little weak, he will keep the prospective disciple in his company for some time, first become convinced about his purity of purpose, and then give him the *mantra*. The *madhyama-adhikārī* Vaiṣṇava mostly acts as *guru*, not the *uttama-adhikārī*. An *uttama-adhikārī* Vaiṣṇava must come down a little to the *madhyama-adhikārī* stage in order to act as *guru*; but the *uttama-adhikārī* generally does not initiate disciples. Nārada became the *guru* of many persons, but he never actually performed the rituals of a formal initiation ceremony. He would simply inspire the flow of *bhakti* in someone's heart, give some instruction, and nothing more.

Once there was a man named Kabīra who wanted to take initiation from a Rāmānuja Vaiṣṇava named Rāmānanda Ācārya. Whenever he would come asking for initiation, Rāmānanda would send him away. Rāmānanda considered this Kabīra to be a first-class *māyāvādī*, a *nirviśeṣavādī*, and therefore thought that he shouldn't be given initiation. So, one night, when it was extremely dark and Rāmānanda was going to bathe, Kabīra, knowing that he was coming, lay down on the path in front of him. Because of the darkness, Rāmānanda did not see Kabīra lying there and tripped over him. Thinking that he had offended someone by touching them with his feet, he said, "Say Rāma! Say Rāma!"

Then, standing up and clasping Rāmānanda's feet, Kabīra said, "This is my initiation, Gurujī. Now you are my *guru*. Rāma, Rāma, Rāma..."

One can get initiated by this kind of trickery also, but we cannot obtain devotion in this way. Kabīra simply remained a first-class *māyāvādī*.

Gopa-kumāra was saying such things that it inspired full faith in the *brāhmaṇa*. The *brāhmaṇa* said, "I have come from afar, and in my heart there is a strong desire to know one thing: what is *sādhya*, the final goal, and *sādhana*, the method to attain it?"

If this question is not within a disciple, then he will never reach the desired goal. When Mahāprabhu was in East Bengal, Tapana Miśra asked Him, "What is our *sādhya* and *sādhana*?" By asking this question, a disciple will please his *guru* very much, and the *guru* will reply, "Oh, what a beautiful question you have asked!"

A disciple will be thinking, "Until now I have been unable to ascertain what our *sādhya* is. Who should we worship, and how should we perform that worship? What is our necessity? To whom will we go, and how will we get to Him?"

Therefore, from the very beginning of our spiritual practice, we must know what is *sādhana* and what is *sādhya*: "Which path should I take? And by travelling along this path, what will I attain?" This knowledge is given only in a real *sampradāya*; in some *sampradāyas* we don't even find this.

Gopa-kumāra said to the *brāhmaṇa*, "My dear friend, there is little time. I will tell you some things regarding this from my own experience. You already possess the *mantra*, and you have already obtained the *darśana* of Mahādeva and Pārvatī-devī. It is possible, in some circumstances, that the *mantra* alone will give you everything. But without remaining in the appropriate Vaiṣṇava association, it is generally not possible to learn the answer to your question. Therefore, in very simple language I will help you to understand what is *sādhya* and *sādhana*. I will tell you in sequence, one stage after the other. If I immediately tell you about *vraja-prema*, the *prema* of the *gopīs*, the *prema* of Rādhikā, or if I immediately tell you how Śrī Kṛṣṇa – Nanda-nandana, Naṭavara, Śyāmasundara, Rādhā-kānta – is alone our most worshipful deity, you will not understand. If I tell you first about the intimate pastimes of Śrī Rādhā and Kṛṣṇa, you will not understand. So I will explain the gradation involved, and according to your specific internal nature you will catch a particular sentiment."

Then Gopa-kumāra began his own life story: "I took birth in the home of a milkman at Govardhana. When I was a little grown up, my parents would send me to take the cows for grazing. Taking the cows out to graze, drinking milk and playing with my friends: it was the carefree life of a young cowherd boy. My friends and I were fearless; we could even fight without fear of being rebuked. The relationships between people there were real and intimate, and this is how I grew up.

"One day I saw a *brāhmaṇa*, and he was very merciful to me. He was always performing *kīrtana* of the name of Bhagavān, and I saw that he was very renounced, never caring for anything of this world. I began to develop some faith in him. My mother would tell me to take him some milk, and I would go and deliver it to him. I told him that whenever he became hungry, he should tell us. While taking the cows out every day, I would go to see him, and slowly I came to love him. Eventually I loved him with my whole heart and soul, so much so that I forgot the affection of my mother and father and everyone else.

"I saw him in many different states – sometimes laughing,

sometimes running, and sometimes rolling on the banks of the Yamunā shouting, 'Hā Kṛṣṇa! Hā Kṛṣṇa!' Witnessing this, great faith in him arose within me. My relationship with the *brāhmaṇa* was very sweet. Like a mother I would sometimes bring him *roṭīs* and other things, but mostly he would take milk. When I would come and sit before him, he would put his hand on my head, pat me on the back and show me great affection. As a result of this, slowly I became indifferent to the things of this world, and I desired to receive initiation from him.

"Then one day I insisted that he initiate me. He told me to first go and bathe in the Yamunā. I did so, and upon returning, he spoke the *mantra* into my ear, the same *mantra* that Pārvatī-devī has given you. Then my *gurudeva* began to tell me the rules and regulations for chanting. He said, 'Who is the deity of this *mantra*? And by chanting it, what kind of sentiment will come into your heart? Listen: with the flute in His hands and a peacock feather on His head, the incomparably marvellous Śyāmasundara...' Then at that moment he became overwhelmed with *bhāva* and fell to the ground unconscious, without having said a word about the rules and regulations or *sādhya* and *sādhana*. He had only told me the *mantra*; he didn't tell me its meaning, or how many times to chant it, or even how to sit while chanting. There was foam coming from his mouth, his limbs were shivering, and the hairs of his body stood erect. I ran to the Yamunā for water to revive him, but when I returned he was no longer there. I searched through all of the *kuñjas* of the entire area of Vṛndāvana. Searching and searching I became exhausted, and not finding him anywhere, I became very upset."

When I received initiation from my *guru*, Śrīla Bhakti Prajñāna Keśava Mahārāja, I also asked him, "Please tell me a little of the meaning of the *gopāla-mantra* and *kāma-gāyatrī*." He replied, "Śrī Rādhā and Kṛṣṇa are the *gopāla-mantra* and *kāma-gāyatrī*. By chanting them, Rādhā and Kṛṣṇa will eventually reveal Themselves to you. There is no necessity of knowing the full meaning now. When the appropriate time comes, the *mantras* will appear within your heart and reveal everything to you." I have always followed his instruction in this regard and there has never been any necessity for me to ask anyone else.

Chapter Two

Gopa-kumāra's Remarkable Journey

Gopa-kumāra's *guru* had disappeared, but his firm faith (*niṣṭhā*) never left him. He never thought of going in a different direction. Whatever the *guru* tells us is the supreme truth of the Vedas, and we should always keep it with us. A *sādhaka* may desire to understand everything by relying solely upon his own experience and then moving forward. Rather than accepting what anyone else may tell him, he may feel that he must directly experience everything himself. But the *guru* can see that trying to understand everything step by step may take millions of lives. What is heaven? What is Siddhaloka? What are Bhūr, Bhuvar, Svar, Mahar, Jano and Tapolokas? What kind of things can be seen there, and what kinds of enjoyment are available? What happiness is there within the eight material coverings? What is in Śivaloka? What is in Vaikuṇṭhaloka? What is in Rāmaloka? We may desire to see and understand all of this by our own endeavour and then consider and accept the highest thing. But one does not progress this way.

For instance, there may be some worldly man who doesn't practise any *sādhana*. We will say to him, "My friend, performing *bhajana* of Bhagavān is the most beneficial thing for you. Leave everything else behind and simply engage in *bhajana*."

So the man may think, "But what about the love of my parents? And I have not yet married – I want to have a little experience of family life."

If he has sufficient merit (*sukṛti*) from previous lifetimes, then he might leave his home; but for those who don't have this previous merit, it will be very difficult. Therefore we can understand that those who have left their families to engage in *bhajana* with great determination have *sukṛti* from their previous births. There is no necessity for them to become involved in family life. Great devotees like Śukadeva Gosvāmī and Nārada Ṛṣi had this previous merit. Generally, by observing someone's activities, we can discern whether they have this *sukṛti* or not.

Many people want to experience all of the many worlds themselves, but not everyone will have the previous merit to do so. Therefore, being merciful, Sanātana Gosvāmī has explained the happiness to be attained in those worlds, the situation there, and the reason for ultimately becoming indifferent to one world and going to another. He revealed all of this through the medium of the story of Gopa-kumāra, taking us through all of those worlds until we finally arrive in Goloka Vṛndāvana.

But we mustn't think that Sanātana Gosvāmī has merely composed a fictitious novel describing Gopa-kumāra's extensive journey; this book contains a wide variety of *siddhānta* with very deep meaning. For example, some people think that the main reason Kṛṣṇa comes to this world is to relieve the Earth's burden. But really He comes to give pleasure to His devotees, and especially to broadcast to the world the *prema* of the *gopīs* and to taste it Himself. Caitanya Mahāprabhu would accomplish many purposes by one activity. He would perform one activity, but from that, five people would be instructed, and five separate objectives would be achieved. In the same spirit Sanātana Gosvāmī has presented the *Bṛhad-bhāgavatāmṛta*.

Gopa-kumāra continued his story: "I was very upset at the loss of my *guru*. By the influence of chanting my *mantra* I felt deep spiritual longing and therefore left my home and family. At Prayaga, I saw a *brāhmaṇa* engaged in worshipping his *śālagrāma-śilā* on the banks of the Gaṅgā. I thought that I would also like to do this, but when I saw him place his *śilā* in a box, I thought, 'If

Ṭhākurajī is placed in a box, He will have to go to sleep hungry, and He won't be able to move either!' It gave me some pain and unhappiness to see this.

"On the advice of that *brāhmaṇa*, I went to the king of Kerala in South India, who was engaged there in worshipping the deity of four-armed Padmanābha with great opulence. He was also feeding, serving and providing all conveniences to the Vaiṣṇavas. Witnessing the opulence of that worship, I stayed there for some time with great love. I was thinking that I also would like to serve the deity as the king was doing. Then the king died with no heir, and the court astrologers found the signs of a king on my hand, so I was made the king and carried on the worship. But whenever the deity's *prasāda* was touched by a person from a lower caste, no one would eat it. People would also accept or reject the *prasāda* on the basis of whether it was cooked or uncooked, and I was very unhappy to see all of this. The *prasāda* of the deity is spiritual, and there should be no such considerations. Therefore I began to feel indifferent towards that place.

"From some Vaiṣṇavas I heard the glories of Śrī Jagannātha. They said, 'In Nīlācala there are no such considerations about *prasāda*. Even if the *prasāda* has been touched by the mouth of a dog, it will still be taken. Regardless of whether it is dry, stale or rotten, it is still considered to be non-different from Bhagavān Himself.'

"So I went there, and upon seeing this I was very pleased. After taking *darśana* of Jagannātha for some time, I began to desire to serve Him in the same manner as the king there. I thought that I would like to become the king myself so I could serve the deity with my own hands. Then the king died, and there was no qualified person to succeed him. His oldest son had left home to engage in *bhajana*, and the younger son didn't possess the necessary signs of a king. The people were in anxiety about who would inherit the throne, so they prayed to Jagannātha. He revealed to them in a dream, 'The throne should be entrusted to whoever has the signs of a king on his hands and feet. The proper signs must be there, and they cannot be cut in any way. Someone may have the proper signs, but they may be cut. He who has the unbroken signs of a flower, waterpot, star and conchshell should be made the king.'

"Seeing these signs on my hands alone, they installed me on the throne. I carried on the deity's service for some time and was very happy. But ultimately I began to feel detached from that place. I saw that the *pujārīs* were always fighting amongst themselves, and sometimes I could not see the deity because the *mandira* was closed, and this caused me to feel great separation. Also Lord Jagannātha never spoke to me. I was chanting my *gopāla-mantra*, and I desired to have the *darśana* of that Gopāla who plays freely and independently with the *gopas*. I was unable to embrace Jagannātha and have such free dealings with Him as I desired.

"Then one day I saw my spiritual master receiving *darśana* in the temple, but he was so overwhelmed with emotion that I could not approach him. He was just gazing at Jagannātha. Thinking that I would speak with him later, I looked away, but when I looked again Gurujī had vanished. I was again upset at losing him. The following day, while wandering on the shores of the ocean, I saw him seated there. There was foam on his mouth and tears in his eyes as he was saying 'Kṛṣṇa, Kṛṣṇa.' After bringing him to external consciousness, I fell at his feet, and then he told me the purport of the *mantra* and some regulations for chanting it. He said, 'This *mantra* will bestow whatever one desires. If you desire to see Bhagavān Himself or anything else, this *mantra* will fulfil your desire.' After saying a little more he again became absorbed in emotion, and where he went after that, I don't know."

Which *mantra* is this? The *gopāla-mantra*. Although at present our faith may not be fully developed, just see how much power is contained within the *gopāla-mantra*!

Gopa-kumāra continued, "My faith increased by hearing just these few words from him, and with great love I chanted my *mantra*. At that time I was feeling indifferent to Nīlācala, and then I heard from some sages that in the heavenly planets Indra is serving Bhagavān directly."

Chanting his *mantra-japa*, intense hankering for going there arose within him, and he immediately arrived in Indraloka. There Indra was directly serving Upendra (Vāmanadeva) delectable foods and drinks like a loving brother. By the influence of his *mantra-japa*, Gopa-kumāra's desire to attain the position of Indra was fulfilled. When Indra fled out of fear of the demons, the sages and demigods appointed him to the position of Indra. For some time he enjoyed the facilities that came with that position and served Upendra in various ways. But during the night he was unable to have Upendra's *darśana*, and for this reason he began to feel indifferent towards that place as well. Next Gopa-kumāra travelled throughout the Bhūr, Bhuvar and Svar planetary systems, having conversations with Pippalāyana and other sages. After that he went to Brahmaloka, where, after some time, he attained the position of Brahmā.

There the personified Vedas, Upaniṣads, Purāṇas and other scriptures were debating amongst themselves. Some were propounding merging into Brahman while others were advocating *bhagavad-bhakti*. They were trying to decide which of the two is superior and whom should be worshipped. At first *Śrīmad-Bhāgavatam* remained neutral and merely listened as they all debated. But in the end the words of the *Bhāgavatam* were established as the best, and the glories of Śrī Viṣṇu and Vaikuṇṭha were delineated.

Again feeling indifferent to his surroundings, Gopa-kumāra chanted his *mantra-japa* and returned to the Vṛndāvana of this world, where he again met his *guru*, Jayanta. Jayanta blessed him, saying, "What you have seen until now is due to the influence of your *mantra*, and by continuing to chant you will also be able to cross the eight material coverings. You will be able to cross the Virajā river and go to Siddhaloka. I am giving you my blessings that you will receive a body that will be suitable for travelling to all of those higher worlds, because no one can go there in a material body. The desires of your heart will surely be fulfilled, but in the course of your journey you mustn't ever stop. Ultimately you will reach your desired goal by going in sequence, step by step."

There is a related story about a sage of Dandakaranya who was performing austerities. He was chanting the *gopāla-mantra* for thousands of years, yet he remained in this world. Eventually Śrī Rāmacandra and Sītā-devī arrived in Dandakaranya. Seeing the beauty of Rāma, the sage's mind became attracted. He prayed to Rāma, "I beg that just as Sītā is serving You, I may serve You in Your form as Gopāla. Please grant me this benediction."

Rāma said, "All right, so it shall be, but you cannot go to Goloka directly. When the pastimes of Kṛṣṇa appear in this universe, you will enter the womb of a *gopī* of Vraja and develop your identity there. You will marry and have a husband, mother-in- law, father-in-law and sister-in-law, but in a hidden way your first love will always be for Gopāla. By the influence of the *gopīs*' association you will attain perfection, and any doubts or ignorance that you may have will vanish. You will appear in the womb of a *gopī*, you will develop an identity within the *līlā*, your sentiment will become perfected, and when Kṛṣṇa and His associates disappear from this world, you will accompany them to Goloka Vṛndāvana and become an eternal companion of Kṛṣṇa. This is the path."

As long as our sentiment is not perfected, we will remain in the Vraja of this world. After attaining perfection we will leave this world; Bhagavān Himself has said this thousands of times. Now we are proceeding along the path step by step and, by the mercy of *guru*, when the appropriate time comes we will obtain a body suitable for travel to higher worlds; but the material body is not able to go there.

Gopa-kumāra appeared the same as before, but at this time he shed his material form and assumed a purely spiritual form. Now like electricity he crossed in one minute the eight material coverings that before had taken him millions of years to cross step by step. The denizens of the heavenly planets showered flowers on him as he passed by at great speed, and Lord Brahmā and others offered obeisances to him. Crossing those eight coverings he saw whatever happiness was available inside them, and then crossing the Virajā he arrived in Śivaloka.

Brahmaloka consists of two sections: the upper part is called Sadāśivaloka, and the lower part is Siddhaloka, which is the destination given to the demons who are personally killed by Bhagavān. The impersonalists also attain this destination after meditating on the formless light for millions of years. That is called *sāyujya-mukti*. This lower part is also called Mahākālapuram or Sāyujyaloka by the sages. This Mahākālapuram is where Kṛṣṇa took Arjuna to retrieve the son of the *brāhmaṇa*.[1]

When Gopa-kumāra was at this Siddhaloka, he saw that it was like a very deep river where one remains submerged in Brahman for some time and then rises up again. By chanting his *gopāla-mantra* he would come up, but then by the influence of the lower world he would again be submerged. Looking upon this formless void with abhorrence, he proceeded up from Siddhaloka to Sadāśivaloka. There Śaṅkara and Pārvatī were performing *kīrtana* and dancing with their associates. Pārvatī is also known as Gaurī, she who possesses a bright bodily complexion. Her limbs were shining like pure camphor and making her appear very beautiful. She was playing some musical instruments and Śaṅkara was dancing. Gaṇeśa was singing, and Kārttikeya, Nandī, Bhṛṅgī and

1 This pastime is narrated in *Śrīmad-Bhāgavatam*, Tenth Canto, Chapter 89.

all of their associates were present there, glorifying Bhagavān and dancing. At that time Gaṇeśa told Gopa-kumāra that Śaṅkara and Bhagavān are one and the same, non-different. After some time, Gopa-kumāra looked up into the sky and saw four people there performing *kīrtana*. They were eternal residents of Vaikuṇṭha. Seeing Śiva and Pārvatī, they offered obeisances and said, "O Mahādeva, you and Hari are the same Soul."

Hearing this, Śiva put his hands over his ears and said, "What are you saying? You don't know any *tattva*. Me – the *īśvara*? No, I am not Íśvara, I am the servant of Íśvara, the servant of Nārāyaṇa."

After those four residents of Vaikuṇṭha elucidated some *tattva*, Śiva began speaking to Gopa-kumāra: "Who can go to Vaikuṇṭha? After one hundred births of giving charity, performing pious activities, and following *varṇāśrama-dharma* perfectly, one attains the position of Brahmā. Then, by performing the function of Brahmā well for one hundred births, one becomes Śiva. After assuming the post of Śiva for thousands of years, one becomes a Vaiṣṇava. I also desire to become a Vaiṣṇava. Then, by practising *sādhana-bhakti* as a Vaiṣṇava, one attains Vaikuṇṭha. Therefore attaining Vaikuṇṭha is not easy; it is very rare. It appears that you are ready to enter Vaikuṇṭha, but you cannot go straight there from here; there is no direct path. From here go to Vraja, engage in some *bhajana* and *sādhana*, and then you can go there."

Chanting his *gopāla-mantra*, Gopa-kumāra saw that he had arrived at Vṛndāvana in the very same *kuñja* near Keśī-ghāṭa where he had previously met his *guru*. There he immersed himself in *sādhana-bhajana*, and one day he was reunited with his *guru* Jayanta. With great *prema* in his heart Jayanta began to tell him some deep secrets, and Gopa-kumāra was very pleased. What kind of secrets? Related to progress in *sādhana-bhajana*: "Your favourite deity is Gopāla, and you are worshipping Him in the mood of fraternity (*sakhya-bhāva*). Until now you have been chanting the *gopāla-mantra*, but in Vaikuṇṭha that *mantra* will no longer be effective. There is no *sādhana* there; it is a place of *sādhya*, final attainment. Therefore, all of the branches of *sādhana* that you have practised up until now will not be effective there. Now your internal identity (*svarupa*) as a *sakhā* has arisen. You are related to Kṛṣṇa as His beloved friend."

The *mantra* had cleansed all kinds of *anartha* and *aparādha* from Gopa-kumāra's heart and established his eternal relationship with Bhagavān. This is such an exalted achievement. The eternal relationship with Kṛṣṇa that we achieve in our hearts will be in whichever *rasa* we find tasteful. As long we do not possess pure attachment to Kṛṣṇa, our *bhajana* will not be pure. Especially for coming to the stage of *rāgānuga-bhakti* this sentiment is so necessary: "Kṛṣṇa is mine, and I am His." At this stage none of the troubles of the material world can disturb us. In the stage of *bhāva* these troubles may come, but in the stage of *prema* we will not be aware of these troubles and they cannot touch us, just as in the cases of Śukadeva Gosvāmī, Nārada Ṛṣi and Prahlāda. But some difficulty came to Bhārata Mahārāja[2], who was only in the stage of *bhāva*, and he was overwhelmed. So in the stage of *bhāva* some troubles may still come, but after that, like the wind they will all fly away and we will not even be aware of them. Then no *anartha*, result of *karma*, or anything unpalatable will come, and in our eternal form we will relish our eternal relationship with Kṛṣṇa.

Then Jayanta secretly told Gopa-kumāra this *mantra*:

śrī-kṛṣṇa gopāla hare mukunda
govinda he nanda-kiśora kṛṣṇa
hā śrī-yaśodā-tanaya prasīda
śrī-ballavī-jīvana rādhikeśa

Bṛhad-bhāgavatāmṛta (2.4.7)

---

2 The story of Bhārata Mahārāja is narrated in *Śrīmad-Bhāgavatam*, Fifth Canto, Chapters 7–8.

In this *mantra*, for Gopa-kumāra the emphasis was on *hā śrī-yaśodā-tanaya prasīda* (O son of Yaśodā), which for him is the primary name of Kṛṣṇa, the others being secondary. For his particular internal sentiment, Yaśodā-tanaya is primary because He is Gopa-kumāra's dear friend, while the remaining names are descriptions: Śrī Kṛṣṇa, Gopāla, Hari, Mukunda, Govinda, Nanda-kiśora, Śrī Ballavī-jīvana and Rādhikeśa. If someone's sentiment is in *mādhurya-rasa*, then Rādhikeśa (the Lord of Rādhā) may be the primary name, and the rest will be secondary.

According to the sentiment in one's heart, one of these names will be selected as the primary name. Śrī Yaśodā-tanaya can be the primary name for both *sakhya-rasa* and *vātsalya-rasa*, the parental mellow. In *mādhurya-rasa*, two names are primary: Śrī Ballavī-jīvana (He who is the very life of the *gopīs*) and Rādhikeśa. Within the name Śrī Ballavī-jīvana a *bhāva* is hidden – a very important, deep *bhāva*. To some devotees, the name Rādhikeśa will not be given; to them the name Śrī Ballavī-jīvana will be given. If a devotee has no desire to become a *sakhī*, but wants instead to become a *mañjarī* and render service that assists the amorous pastimes of Śrī Rādhā-Kṛṣṇa from that position, then the name Śrī Ballavī-jīvana is given to them. But those who chant Rādhikeśa will become *sakhīs*. As we progress in *sādhana* we will be able to better understand these subtle points.

Jayanta didn't tell these secret things to just anyone, only to Gopa-kumāra. Then, while Gopa-kumāra was looking the other way, Jayanta vanished again. With dazzling effulgence and the speed of electricity he would appear, tell Gopa-kumāra one or two things, and then disappear. But we are so fortunate that we have been given the opportunity to spend so much time in the personal company of our *guru*. Every day we speak with him and he gives us personal instruction and everything. Therefore we are not really such qualified recipients. If we were, then shining like electricity the spiritual master would appear and give us one or two relevant thoughts, which we would keep with us for all time; then he would vanish. Like feeding us milk – have you seen a dog with her puppies? She comes and feeds them milk, and when she again leaves from there, the puppies race after her. But she nudges them away and proceeds, leaving them standing at a distance just watching, and then finally they return home. Like this, the *guru* will come, nurture the sentiment of a disciple by giving some relevant instruction, and then vanish.

After residing in Vṛndāvana and performing *bhajana* for some time, Gopa-kumāra became absorbed in *prema*. Then one day he beheld the most wondrous vision: wearing yellow cloth, playing the flute, smiling and speaking to him with His eyes, Śrī Kṛṣṇa was suddenly present before him. Gopa-kumāra cried out, "Oh! My very life!" and raced after Him. Coming near to Kṛṣṇa he tried to embrace Him, but just then Kṛṣṇa disappeared. Crying and crying in deep separation, Gopa-kumāra fell to the ground unconscious. While in his unconscious state, he saw a beautiful golden airplane appear before him at the speed of mind. Inside it were those same four residents of Vaikuṇṭha whom he had met in Śivaloka and who had spoken some *tattva* to him. They said, "Please come; now we are proceeding to Vaikuṇṭha."

Mostly still in an unconscious state, Gopa-kumāra stood up and sat inside the airplane. When he opened his eyes he thought, "Where am I? What is this place?" He found himself in a waiting room at the gates of Vaikuṇṭha. His guardians told him, "Please wait here. We are going inside to obtain the order from the Lord, and then we will take you inside."

Saying this they went inside, and took quite some time to return. During this time Gopa-kumāra saw, one after another, many eternal associates of Bhagavān entering through the gates. They were carrying presents and paraphernalia for the *pūjā* of

Nārāyaṇa. Seeing their shining effulgence, he mistook one of them to be Nārāyaṇa Himself, and offering his *praṇāma* said, "O Nārāyaṇa, O Lord, please be merciful to me!"

That devotee replied, "Oh! Don't call me Nārāyaṇa! I am not Nārāyaṇa; I am only the servant of the servant of Nārāyaṇa." Everyone that came was greeted by Gopa-kumāra in the same manner. He was wonderstruck at the opulence of Vaikuṇṭha. He saw monkeys, bears, peacocks and other kinds of birds arriving there, and they all appeared divinely beautiful. Then the four Vaiṣṇavas who had brought him returned and said, "Come, the Lord has given His order."

Upon entering through the gates and seeing the opulence of the doorman, Gopa-kumāra mistook him to be Nārāyaṇa as well and began to offer him obeisances and prayers. The doorman put his hands over his ears and the party proceeded further until they reached an interior chamber. There, accompanied by Lakṣmī-devī herself and with Nārada and other sages at His side, was Śrī Nārāyaṇa, reclining to one side on His elbow. He was chewing betel nuts and appeared very splendid. Gopa-kumāra offered *praṇāma*, and Nārāyaṇa raised His hand in bestowal of blessings and said, "You have given Me so much suffering. For millions of years I have been waiting for you, thinking, 'When will he come to Me?' Millions of years have passed, and until now I could not find any pretext to bring you here to Vaikuṇṭha. I was very upset about this, but I saw that you didn't have even a little desire to meet Me. If you had only chanted even one of My names just once, kept association with My devotees or offered some service to a saint – but you did nothing at all. Even if you had circumambulated a temple just once! One particular pigeon did, and I awarded him entrance into My abode. I could have done the same for you. A hunter with a bow and arrow shot this pigeon who was seated on the branch of a tree, and the bird fell to the ground. In its wounded condition, unintentionally, the pigeon circumambulated the temple one time before dying. From that it attained enough merit to take a human birth and begin voluntarily associating with My devotees. Then in its next birth it came to Me.

"There was also one mouse who entered a *mandira* to drink ghee. The ghee lamp was flickering, almost extinguished, and just then this mouse began drinking some ghee from it. By this movement the lamp became lit again, and the mouse ran off, frightened. From this he attained the result of offering a lamp to the deity. In his next life he took a human birth and then gradually, by the mercy of the Vaiṣṇavas, he attained Vaikuṇṭha. But you didn't even do anything like this. All of the time you were opposed to Me. You remained in bad company, always spoke about mundane topics and you were always absorbed in sense enjoyment. You never did anything to bring yourself in My direction. I thought, 'By any means I must save him.' So I arranged for you to take birth at Govardhana and then I Myself came as your *guru*: that was none other – that was Me. I gave you the *gopāla-mantra*, and then I kept coming in the midst of your progress to nourish your *mantra* and strengthen your *sādhana*.

"One will not meet such a *guru* in one or two lives, but only after thousands of births will one receive a *guru* who can lead him to Me. I came to you in many forms and gave you inspiration, instilled spiritual strength within you and told you all of the deep secrets of *bhajana*. Now, it is very good that we have finally met, and I am very happy! You will stay here now and not go anywhere else."

Gopa-kumāra began staying there. One day Lakṣmī-devī saw that evening was approaching and everyone had left the presence of Nārāyaṇa except Gopa-kumāra. Since Lakṣmī-devī alone serves Nārāyaṇa food and drink and massages His feet, she told Viśvaksena and others to employ some cleverness to draw Gopa-kumāra away. They said to him, "Come and take rest, it is late.

Everyone is going, and you also need rest; you appear very tired. Therefore please come with us and take some rest." They tried this trickery to draw Gopa-kumāra away, but he didn't desire to go. Finally they affectionately took his hand and led him away, but this made him very unhappy.

Another day Nārāyaṇa called Gopa-kumāra and said, "Come and do the service of fanning Me." Gopa-kumāra became very pleased upon obtaining this service, but what did he really want? "I desire to play the flute with Him, embrace Him and take *prasāda* directly from His plate. I want to take the cows out to graze with Him and accompany Him to His house, where His mother will feed us and give us nice things to drink. I want this type of free and independent relationship with Nārāyaṇa, but He will not reciprocate with me in the same way. Instead, here I am bound up: with my hands together I must offer *praṇāma*." Thinking like this, Gopa-kumāra became even more unhappy.

One day Nārada approached him and said, "Your face appears withered in unhappiness. I can see that you are not satisfied." Even before Gopa-kumāra could reply, Nārada had understood everything. Beginning to speak, Nārada felt a little shy because Lakṣmī-devī and others were nearby and he could not speak openly before them. So he took Gopa-kumāra to a solitary place, and said, "Aho! Inside you there is some very deep yearning? Here you don't have the relationship with Bhagavān that you long for. You desire *sakhya-bhāva*. Here Bhagavān will not kiss and embrace you; you cannot eat from the same plate with Him and sleep on the same bed. All these loving exchanges of *sakhya-bhāva* are what you really desire. This has been your strong desire for a very long time.

"In this place your desire will not be fulfilled, but don't be discouraged, because there is one thing you must understand: Nārāyaṇa is your worshipful Lord. He and the Gopāla that you desire in *sakhya-bhāva* are one and the same, non-different. Silently you are longing to play with Him in *sakhya-bhāva*, but here that longing will not be fulfilled. I will tell you how to proceed upwards to your next destination."

Chapter Three

The Superiority of Nāma-saṅkīrtana

In telling Gopa-kumāra the *sādhana* for attaining Vaikuṇṭha, the four-armed eternal associates of Nārāyaṇa said:

manyāmahe kīrtanam eva sattamaṁ
lokātmakaika-sva-hṛdi smarat smṛteḥ
vāci sva-yukte manasi śrutau tathā
dīvyat parān apy apakurvad ātmya-vat
Bṛhad-bhāgavatāmṛta (2.3.148)

Because it engages the voice, ears and mind, and because it attracts others as it does oneself, we consider that *kīrtana* is better than trying to remember the Lord with the fickle mind.

There are so many kinds of *sādhana* for attaining Vaikuṇṭha, and this refers to the entire realm of Vaikuṇṭha, up to Vṛndāvana. For everyone in a general way, it is said that there are many *sādhanas* for attaining Vaikuṇṭha, such as ninefold *bhakti*, fivefold *bhakti*, sixty-four kinds of *bhakti* and so on. Amongst all of these, three are primary: hearing (*śravaṇa*), chanting (*kīrtana*) and remembering (*smaraṇa*). Of these three, *kīrtana* and *smaraṇa* are primary. What is the meaning of *smaraṇa*? Rūpa Gosvāmī says it means that while your tongue is chanting your favourite name of Bhagavān, your mind is remembering Kṛṣṇa's pastimes.

In our *sampradāya* there are many who consider that, leaving aside all other methods, only meditation (*dhyāna*) should be done. Especially for developing *rāgānuga-bhakti*, meditating on the topics of Kṛṣṇa's pastimes and remembering His eternal eightfold daily pastimes (*aṣṭakāla-līlā*) have been recommended as the best type of *smaraṇa*. But here Sanātana Gosvāmī, through the medium of Gopa-kumāra and the four-armed eternal associates of Nārāyaṇa, is saying that *saṅkīrtana* is the best method of all. Why? Because the mind is restless; it won't remain steady. If anyone can deeply meditate on the pastimes of Kṛṣṇa with a steady mind, then that is all right. But in almost every situation the mind is not peaceful; it remains restless. Therefore there is only one plan (*Śrīmad-Bhāgavatam* 11.2.40):

evaṁ-vrataḥ sva-priya-nāma-kīrtyā
jātānurāgo druta-citta uccaiḥ

With a melted heart, loudly sing about the names, forms, qualities and pastimes of Bhagavān. When one sincerely chants his favourite name of Bhagavān, then from the tongue that name will enter the mind and then the heart, thereby quieting all of the senses. If by any separate endeavour one tries to control the restless mind, he will not be able to do so. For concentrating the mind, *kīrtana* is necessary, and especially for Kali-yuga, Śrī Caitanya Mahāprabhu has given us *nāma-saṅkīrtana* as the religion for the modern age (*yuga-dharma*):

harer nāma harer nāma
harer nāmaiva kevalam
kalau nāsty eva nāsty eva
nāsty eva gatir anyathā

Bṛhan-nāradīya Purāṇa (38.126)

> In Kali-yuga, *hari-kīrtana* is the only means of deliverance. There is no other way.

Only *nāma-saṅkīrtana* will make the restless mind steady, and is therefore the best method of all. If one performs *smaraṇa* that is dependent on *kīrtana*, then that will be effective. Arising on the tongue, *nāma-saṅkīrtana* will control all of the remaining senses and the mind also; otherwise the mind is like a horse without a rider. If there are no reins and no rider, what will the horse do? Run here and there according to his own desire. But if the rider of *kīrtana* climbs upon the horse of our mind and takes the reins, then the horse of the mind will not run aimlessly but will go wherever the rider directs him. So what the four-armed eternal associates of Nārāyaṇa were saying was conducive for the cultivation of *bhakti*, and ultimately for gaining entrance into Vraja. For this reason Jayanta gave Gopa-kumāra this *mantra* to chant:

śrī-kṛṣṇa gopāla hare mukunda
govinda he nanda-kiśora kṛṣṇa
hā śrī-yaśodā-tanaya prasīda
śrī-ballavī-jīvana rādhikeśa

We have heard that anyone who doesn't perform *kīrtana* that is full of the names of Bhagavān, but only chants the *gopāla-mantra*, will not be able to enter Goloka Vraja. But it has also been said that the sixty thousand sages who witnessed the pastimes of Rāma in Satya-yuga performed *sādhana* by chanting the *gopāla-mantra*, and as a result they attained the forms of *gopīs* in their next lives. And those who cite this reference say, "So how can the *gopāla-mantra* be considered inferior? The *kāma-gāyatrī* is inferior? They will not take one to Goloka? The *gopāla-mantra* and the *kāma-gāyatrī* are *mantras* of perfection! Anyone who performs *sādhana* by chanting them will certainly attain Goloka!"

How can we harmonise this? Harmonising this seems to be a very difficult task because it appears that there is a contradiction in our *siddhānta*. Some say that only *nāma-saṅkīrtana* will take us to Goloka, but others have written that by chanting the *gopāla-mantra* so many people went to Goloka Vraja. So how can we reconcile this?

Very easily: where is perfection attained? Where is *sādhana* practised? In this material world, and those sages of Daṇḍakāraṇya were practising *sādhana* by chanting the *gopāla-mantra*. From the *mantra*, *sambandha-jñāna* arose and ultimately transformed into permanent sentiment (*sthāyibhāva*), and according to their particular internal natures, they attained perfection. They reached the limit of this world and became qualified to go beyond. Then, by the influence of Yogamāyā, such perfected souls take birth in the womb of *gopīs* when the manifest pastimes of Kṛṣṇa appear in one of the material universes. After taking birth in Vraja from the womb of a *gopī*, they become either a *sakhā*, a motherly or father like guardian of Kṛṣṇa, or a *gopī*. But they must first take birth in Gokula and develop an identity.

Then there is no necessity of chanting the *mantra* any longer. Rather, by hearing and chanting about Kṛṣṇa's pastimes – and by the association of Gopāla Himself, the *gopīs* and all of His other eternal playmates – one will himself become part of Kṛṣṇa's eternal entourage and then go to Goloka Vṛndāvana. One will not go directly. Therefore everything is reconciled like this: first there is *svarūpa-siddhi*, internal realisation of one's eternal identity, and then after relinquishing the material body comes *vastu-siddhi*, taking birth in a spiritual body within the Lord's pastimes. The *mantra* is only useful in *sādhana*. There is no necessity of it in the stage of perfection.

So, saying that the *gopāla-mantra* will take one to Goloka Vraja is correct: it will bring us to the entrance, and then we will enter and the activities of the *mantra* will cease. Both ideas in regard to the *mantra* are correct. But without the *gopāla-mantra* and the *kāma-gāyatrī*, will our *sādhana* be complete with only *nāma-saṅkīrtana*? No, because by *nāma-saṅkīrtana* alone we will not be able to chant *śuddha-nāma*, the pure name of Kṛṣṇa. First, from the influence of the *mantra, sambandha-jñāna* will come, then we will feel a particular devotional sentiment within us, and finally our eternal *svarūpa* will arise. After this, by becoming deeply absorbed in *nāma-saṅkīrtana*, everything will be completed.

Suppose we are cutting grass, and someone says to us, "Please use a golden blade to cut the grass." Will we use a golden blade to cut the grass? No, an iron blade will be more effective. Similarly, because we are in such a conditioned state, chanting the *gopāla-mantra* and *kāma-gāyatrī* is also necessary. At different stages, different things are necessary, but we shall understand *nāma-saṅkīrtana* to be the best thing in *sādhana*, and in perfection. The *gopāla-mantra* is effective only in *sādhana*, but not in the stage of perfection. The perfected soul will not chant it, because its work has been completed. We must understand this point well: *nāma-saṅkīrtana* is necessary in the conditioned state, but along with it we must chant the *gopāla-mantra*, the *mantra* of Mahāprabhu (*gaura-gāyatrī*), and all other *mantras* that our spiritual master has given us. The efficacy of these *mantras* is that they make *sambandha-jñāna* arise and the attachment to sense enjoyment fade away. Anyone who follows this method sincerely for one year, or even six months, will certainly see what its result is. If the desired result doesn't come, then there must be some problem. Perhaps the seed, the *mantra*, was not very potent because the giver was not pure, or perhaps we are not chanting from the heart or we are cheating in some way. Rather, giving it our heart, with deep faith and firm determination we should chant.

kṛṣṇasya nānā-vidha-kīrtaneṣu
tan-nāma-saṅkīrtanam eva mukhyam
tat-prema-sampaj-janane svayaṁ drāk
śaktaṁ tataḥ śreṣṭhatamaṁ mataṁ tat

Bṛhad-bhāgavatāmṛta (2.3.158)

Of the many types of *kṛṣṇa-kīrtana*, glorification of His name is primary. Because it is capable of bestowing the great wealth of pure love for Him very quickly, it is considered the best.

There are many types of *kṛṣṇa-kīrtana* – glorification of His qualities, of His form, of His pastimes – but the glorification of His name is the foremost. If I call out "Come over here," who will come? Many people may come. If I describe some qualities of the person I want, then still many may come. But if I call out the name of the specific person I want, then at once only that person will come. Similarly, there is glorification of Bhagavān's qualities, forms and pastimes, but for calling out to Him and remembering Him, the *nāma-saṅkīrtana* of Bhagavān is the best. Included within this *nāma-saṅkīrtana* will be glorification of His qualities, forms and pastimes. In this way – "O Govinda, O Gopīnātha, O Madana-mohana!" – our *kīrtana* should be full of His names. And of these names, those which refer to Kṛṣṇa's relationship with the *gopīs* are the best of all. If one desires to very quickly attain the lotus feet of Śrī Kṛṣṇa and attain the *prema* of Vraja, then *nāma-saṅkīrtana* is the best and most powerful method. This is the conclusion of Sanātana Gosvāmī, because if we chant *nāma-saṅkīrtana* with great sincerity, then very quickly *kṛṣṇa-prema* will arise.

nāma-saṅkīrtanaṁ proktaṁ
kṛṣṇasya prema-sampadi
baliṣṭhaṁ sādhanaṁ śreṣṭham
paramākarṣa-mantra-vat

Bṛhad-bhāgavatāmṛta (2.3.164)

It is said that *nāma-saṅkīrtana* is the best and most powerful method for attaining the treasure of *kṛṣṇa-prema* because, like the most supremely magnetic *mantra*, it pulls Śrī Kṛṣṇa towards a *sādhaka*.

Therefore Gopa-kumāra was instructed to again return to the material world where his spiritual master instructed him on *kīrtana*, and gave him this *mantra* to chant:

śrī-kṛṣṇa gopāla hare mukunda
govinda he nanda-kiśora kṛṣṇa
hā śrī-yaśodā-tanaya prasīda
śrī-ballavī-jīvana rādhikeśa

Here, one doubt may arise. Sanātana Gosvāmī and Caitanya Mahāprabhu were contemporary, and at that time the preaching of the *mahā-mantra* was going on. Mahāprabhu had begun the specific propagation of the *mahā-mantra* in Navadvīpa, and in Purī also it was going on. But in his *Bṛhad-bhāgavatāmṛta*, Sanātana Gosvāmī did not write anything in relation to the *mahā-mantra*; instead he gave the *mantra* containing the names *śrī-kṛṣṇa gopāla hare mukunda*..., so should we think he didn't know of the *mahā-mantra*? What was the reason for his not giving the *mahā-mantra*?

The *mahā-mantra* is especially meant for Kali-yuga, whereas this *mantra* from *Bṛhad-bhāgavatāmṛta* is for all time, as are the *gopāla-mantra* and the *gāyatrī-mantra*. But more importantly, Gopa-kumāra had the internal sentiment of a cowherd boy, and therefore more explicit names such as Śrī Yaśodā-tanaya and Nanda-kiśora Kṛṣṇa were given to him. Śrī Caitanya Mahāprabhu and the Gosvāmīs chanted the *mahā-mantra* knowing that ultimately the only meaning of the *mahā-mantra* is Śrī Rādhā-Kṛṣṇa Themselves, but ordinarily one wouldn't see this meaning there. They chanted it with intense feelings of separation full of *rasa* and the sentiments of Vraja. Anyone who comes to know this meaning will definitely prefer chanting the *mahā-mantra* over the *mantra*, *śrī-kṛṣṇa gopāla hare mukunda*... . But because Gopa-kumāra was merely a simple cowherd boy who had no knowledge of *tattva*, he would have been unable to detect the sentiment of Vraja within the *mahā-mantra*.

We cannot see a plant or a tree within a seed but they are there, and an expert can examine a seed and determine whether it will produce one thing or another. Or if there are two pots of yoghurt, one may examine them side by side and determine which one is naturally sweet. The pot of yoghurt that has had sugar added will have a slightly pinkish appearance, and should only cost three rupees per kilo. Why? Because the cream has been removed from this yoghurt, it has been skimmed, and a little sugar has been added to give it some artificial sweetness. But the other pot containing only simple and pure yoghurt with its own natural white colour and sweetness is worth ten rupees per kilo because it has been made from whole milk and therefore there is ghee in every particle of it.

Similarly, the Gosvāmīs have examined the sixteen names in the *mahā-mantra*, extracted the meaning, and tasted it. When chanting the *mahā-mantra*, the deity whom we are aspiring to serve is inherent within the names that we are calling. For instance, in "Hare Rāma", to us the name "Rāma" means only Rādhā-ramaṇa Kṛṣṇa, and "Hare" means Śrīmatī Rādhikā, the one who steals Śrī Kṛṣṇa away to the *kuñja*, gives Him great pleasure, and serves Him with *prema-bhāva*. When chanting "Hare", we are exclusively calling Śrīmatī Rādhikā. If anyone receives this understanding from a *sad-guru* or a *rasika* Vaiṣṇava, and chants the *mahā-mantra* full of this sentiment, then their eternal *svarūpa* will appear within them very soon. Otherwise, if we have received the *mantra* in a crooked way, we will think that its meaning is not Śrī Rādhā-Kṛṣṇa Themselves, but something else.

So in the *Bṛhad-bhāgavatāmṛta*, Sanātana Gosvāmī has given the *mantra, śrī-kṛṣṇa gopāla hare mukunda...* because for some this is necessary, but ordinarily for the *jīvas* of Kali-yuga the *mahā-mantra* has been given, and in accordance with the scriptures it should be firmly adhered to and chanted always.

Chapter Four

The Moods of Intimacy and Sweetness

Although Gopa-kumāra had arrived in Vaikuṇṭha-dhāma, his heart did not feel satisfaction there. I had a similar experience recently in Bombay. We had been invited to stay in the home of a wealthy gentleman there, and upon entering his home, I could not find my way around that place, really. They had a very beautiful floor that was shining like a mirror, and I actually became confused, just as Duryodhana became bewildered in the assembly house of Yudhiṣṭhira Mahārāja. Mahāprabhu and His devotees would not go to the house of any king because the lust of worldly people can be very contaminating. Seeing their opulence, we will begin thinking, "My home should be like this," "My āśrama should be like this." Then, not being able to acquire such things, this lust will intensify within us. So instead we left and stayed in the home of an ordinary family.

In Bombay, there are even people who are millions of rupees more wealthy than that gentleman who had invited us. Therefore, what can be said of the enjoyment available in the heavenly planets? We cannot comprehend such opulence. If we were to go there, we would forget everything of this world. So if we were to go to Vaikuṇṭha, what would we find? There the opulence is even greater. There is such an abundance of happiness there that anyone who enters Vaikuṇṭha will never have a desire to leave. There is so much beauty, and no one ever becomes old or diseased. There is no birth and no death, whereas in heaven there is. Up to Mahar, Jano, Tapo and Satyalokas there is birth and death, but there is no trace of them in Vaikuṇṭha. There is always new and fresh happiness, and opulence of the highest standard. Even the soil there is *cinmaya*, transcendental.

kalpa-taravo drumā bhūmi. cintāmaṇi-gaṇa-mayī
toyam amṛtam kathā gānaṁ naṭyaṁ gamanam api

Brahma-saṁhitā (5.56)

The trees there are desire trees (*kalpataru*), and the land is touchstone (*cintāmaṇi*). The water is nectar, the talking is singing and the walking is dancing – this is the nature of Vaikuṇṭha. But Gopa-kumāra was feeling dissatisfied there, and Nārada said to him, "This is a very grave matter. Here I see that your face is withered in worry. How is this possible? Coming here, no one can remain unhappy, but I see that you are. What is it – is there anything you are lacking, or is something else making you unhappy? What is it?"

Such unhappiness will not be felt by everyone there, but only by a special person. If for any reason someone is unhappy there, they won't be able to express it to anyone. Such intense unhappiness cannot be expressed even to your mother, father, brother or sister, but only to a bosom friend. By some means he will remove the thorn, and he will understand your feelings. Nārada can see inside all souls; he knows everything. With his eyes closed in meditation, he ascertained the reason for Gopa-kumāra's unhappiness and became very pleased. Why is it that seeing such unhappiness in another he became pleased? There is one related story in this connection.

When Uddhava went to Vṛndāvana, he saw that Nanda Mahārāja was wailing in lamentation, crying for Kṛṣṇa. Kṛṣṇa was such a wonderful son, but now leaving Nanda behind, He had gone away. Nanda was very unhappy, but what was Uddhava thinking? "Today, I am supremely fortunate to have received the *darśana* of such an exalted personality who is actually crying for Bhagavān."

In the materially conditioned state of life, everyone is crying for themselves. All for themselves. When a brother dies, for whom is the family crying – for the brother or for themselves? It seems that they are crying for the brother, but really they are not. "If my brother had lived, then he would have given me all sorts of help. Now I am helpless" – this is what they are really crying about. "Father has died; if he had lived, then very easily all of our desires would have been fulfilled." "My wife has died; she was very beautiful and a great servant. Seating us comfortably, she would serve us food, water and everything. Now she is gone," and the husband is left crying, but is he really crying for the wife? Really he is crying for himself.

So if in any situation a father is crying for a son, we can understand that actually he is crying for himself. But what Uddhava had witnessed was Nanda Bābā really crying for Kṛṣṇa, not for himself – such deep *kṛṣṇa-prema* was inside him. We should also aspire to be a little like this. If even one time we shed a tear that is actually for Bhagavān, then our lives will be meaningful. But our hearts are not yet melted, and therefore while chanting the holy name our hair does not stand on end. Mahāprabhu Himself said (*Śrī Śikṣāṣṭaka* 6):

nayanaṁ galad-aśru-dhārayā
vadanaṁ gadgada-ruddhayā girā
pulakair nicitaṁ vapuḥ kadā
tava nāma-grahaṇe bhaviṣyati

O Lord, when, while chanting Your name, will tears flow from my eyes like waves? When will my voice tremble in ecstasy and the hairs of my body stand erect?

What is the meaning of the word *bhaviṣyati*? When will that opportunity come that one day, while chanting *harināma*, tears will come from our eyes in a continuous flow that will never stop? When will we be trembling and feeling our heart melting, sometimes rolling on the ground, sometimes laughing, sometimes crying and sometimes singing? Uddhava witnessed all of this and thought, "Today I am so fortunate to have the *darśana* of such a great personality. But what will I say: 'You are the most fortunate person?' I am unable to say that. Should I tell him to go on crying, or should I try to console him and tell him not to cry? In this world, if a man is crying for Kṛṣṇa, that is actually desirable! I desire to have sentiments like that also! If he is really crying in *kṛṣṇa-prema*, he is the most fortunate person, but how can I say anything? 'Cry' or 'Don't cry' – I cannot say either of those things. What can be done... ."

So Uddhava could not speak even one word to Nanda Bābā. Seeing the divine ecstasy of Nanda Bābā, Uddhava felt that on that day his life had become successful. And a similar sentiment came into the heart of Nārada upon seeing the condition of Gopa-kumāra. "You are so very, very fortunate. Even here in Vaikuṇṭha you are unhappy because you want Nārāyaṇa to be Kṛṣṇa. You want to take the cows out to graze with Him, and you want to live with Him. You want to put your arms around Him and embrace as friends. You want Kṛṣṇa to say, 'Hey, Gopa-kumāra, bring the cows over this way! The cows are thirsty, give them some water!', and with great love you will follow the order of Kṛṣṇa. You want that sometimes Kṛṣṇa will embrace you, and sometimes you will embrace Him. That you will eat together, and even with unclean hands you will place food into each others' mouths. That sometimes, when Kṛṣṇa is sleeping on the bed of Yaśodā, you will arrive at His bedside with your body covered with the dust of Vṛndāvana and say, 'Hey, don't sleep now! The cows have arrived at the door. Let's go!' You want to do all of this, and it can be very easily achieved as a *sakhā*.

"But what does Nārāyaṇa do? When you go before Him, He lifts His right hand in bestowal of blessings: 'May all auspiciousness be upon you.' Saying '*Namo nārāyaṇa, namo nārāyaṇa,*' everyone is offering *praṇāma* to Him. He lifts His hand and gives this blessing: 'You will be fearless. All good fortune shall attend you.' You want to race to embrace Him, and you want to play the flute with Him, but you are not able to do any of this. You desire to sleep on the same bed with Him at night, but by cleverness and trickery, or by some other means, Lakṣmī-devī sends you away. And when you don't leave, what does she do? She calls the doormen Jaya and Vijaya and says, 'He is not obeying me,' and she has you removed. When you sing, 'Śrī Kṛṣṇa! Gopāla! Hare! Mukunda! O Govinda! O Nanda-kiśora! O Kṛṣṇa! O Śrī Yaśodā-tanaya! O Śrī Ballavī-jīvana! O Rādhikeśa! Be merciful to me!' and play the flute and express a desire to take the cows out to graze, all the residents of Vaikuṇṭha abuse you and say, 'Hey, what are you saying? Nārāyaṇa, Prabhu, the Controller of the controllers of all the worlds – you are calling Him Gopāla and say that you will take cows out to graze together? You want to make Him the guardian of cows? You say that He milks cows, that He is the lover of some cowherd women, and the son of a milkman? You say that, entering the home of a milkman together, you and He will steal yoghurt and sweets? You call Him a thief? You are disreputing Him! You should be saying that He is Viṣṇu, who possesses thousands of heads! You should be glorifying Him in the form in which He gives blessings and good fortune to all. How can you say that He is a milkman, a thief and a liar? You shouldn't do this.' Saying this, they all make jokes and laugh at you.

"Some say, 'My friend, it's true that Nārāyaṇa became Kṛṣṇa and for His own pleasure and the amusement of His devotees He performed some pastimes, but those pastimes are not important. This is Vaikuṇṭha, not Vraja. You shouldn't speak of such things here.' Hearing them speak like this, you constantly feel ashamed."

Suppose a cowherd boy such as Śrīdāmā or Subala were to go to Dvārakā to see Kṛṣṇa. They would see that Kṛṣṇa is seated there in the royal Sudharmā assembly house as Dvārakādhīśa, the Mahārāja of Dvārakā. Ugrasena, Vasudeva and all the elders of the Yadu dynasty are seated at His right side. Garga Ṛṣi and many other eminent sages are seated in front of Him. His sons Sāmba, Aniruddha and Pradyumna are seated at His left side, and behind a curtain are Rukmiṇī and Satyabhāmā, along with Devakī and the other queens. Now if some cowherd boy arrives in that assembly, how will he appear? In cowherd dress, with a bent stick in one hand for guiding the cows and a bamboo flute in the other. It will be early evening, and having just returned from taking the cows out for grazing, he will be very dusty and in need of changing his clothes. If he arrives in that assembly, he will want to embrace Kṛṣṇa, but Kṛṣṇa will only sit quietly, glancing at the *gopa* only once and not again.

That poor fellow would have come with such high expectations: the expectation that "Kṛṣṇa, by His quality of *bhakta-vātsalya*, possessing special affection for His devotees, will call me to come and sit near Him." But that would not happen there. Instead, someone would say to him, "My friend, step this way." Then the cowherd boy would see all of the opulence there and think, "Oh! Look at this umbrella, and look at this *cāmara*! Look at all of these people!" Then he would look at himself, feel ashamed, and go away from there. In that place Rukmiṇī, Satyabhāmā and the other ladies are decorated with ornaments as queens, so what would happen if an ordinary lady with flowers in her hair and wearing no costly jewellery went there? Therefore the *gopīs* never go there because they would not be respected.

Nārada was thinking, "This Gopa-kumāra has such a high position that he considers Kṛṣṇa his dear friend, so he will never be satisfied here in Vaikuṇṭha. His eternal identity (*svarūpa*) will not be recognised here; its full glory will not be realised." If any of us are ever fortunate enough to attain the *svarūpa* of a *gopa* or a *gopī*, then if we were to go to heaven or Vaikuṇṭha, we also would not like it there. Perhaps Nārada would come to us, ascertain our internal state, and think to himself, "She is special. She is a servant of Rādhikā." But he wouldn't tell anyone; he would just silently offer respects. He would understand that our eternal identity is not right for that place; the *guru* can always understand.

Similarly, Nārada saw the internal sentiment of Gopa-kumāra, understood the situation, and became very pleased. Then, after thinking about what to say and what not to say, he said, "Hmm... after taking your pulse, I'm thinking that the disease you have is not an ordinary disease. The cure for it cannot be found in Vaikuṇṭha; there is no medicine for it here. And by staying here, the disease will only increase. But I will now tell you how your disease may be cured. You require affection that is free of all reservations. This is called *viśrambha-bhāva*, the mood of intimacy. In Vaikuṇṭha, there is only *sambhrama-bhāva*."

In *Śrī Caitanya-caritāmṛta* (*Ādi-līlā* 4.17) it is said:

aiśvarya-jñānete saba jagat miśrita
aiśvarya-śithila-preme nāhi mora prīta

In Vaikuṇṭha there is *prema*, but it is weakened by Bhagavān's servants' awareness of His majesty, *aiśvarya*. They are serving Him with awareness of all of His opulences, and therefore they are a little fearful. Śrī Rāmacandra is seated on a bed, and Hanumān is seated below. Crouching down, on cold days he will massage the feet of Rāmacandra and cover the Lord with a quilt. He is serving with love and Bhagavān is pleased, but there is a more intimate type of *prema*, called *viśrambha*. The *prema* of Jaya, Vijaya and Lakṣmī-devī is not *viśrambha*; it is *sambhrama*, which means that they are aware of their own insignificance and therefore feel a little fearful. Bhagavān is not fully satisfied by this type of service, but if we try to serve Him with the mood of *viśrambha* in our conditioned state, it will be offensive, although it is written in the scriptures, "*viśrambhena gurau sevā* – in the mood of intimacy we should serve the spiritual master." Here the purport of *viśrambha* is that we should understand the *guru* to be a friend and serve him as we would our mother, father, brother or friend.

When a friend of your family comes to your house, you will not need to be told, "Your friend has come; offer him a nice sitting place and bring him something to drink." Automatically you will do it. Therefore, the topmost (*uttama*) servant will understand his *guru's* desires and automatically act to fulfil them without receiving any specific order. Serving without having to be told – this is a symptom of the servant. One who serves his *guru* after being told is an intermediate (*madhyama*) servant. Then there is one other type of servant to whom the *guru* will say, "Go send for such-and-such Mahārāja."

This servant will answer back, "But Gurujī, now it is early evening and it is becoming dark."

The *guru* knows it is becoming dark, but he has given his order. "It doesn't matter if it is dark; just go!"

Then this servant will say, "But Gurujī, on the road there are many dogs."

"Never mind that – take a stick with you and go!"

"But what if I go and Mahārāja is not there; then what will I do?"

What can such a servant do? From the word *sevaka*, meaning 'servant', remove the *se* and that leaves *vaka*. *Vaka* means 'a crane', a hypocritical devotee. The crane stands in the water on one leg as if he were a great renounced devotee in meditation. But as soon as a fish swims by, he will snatch it and eat it and then return to his pose. Therefore the *uttama* servant is a real servant, and in a general way we can also call the *madhyama* servant a real servant, but one who is argumentative is not a servant at all.

If we don't understand the heart of the *guru*, then how will we understand the heart of Kṛṣṇa? Therefore, those people who desire to go beyond Vaikuṇṭha should serve their spiritual master with *viśrambha* love. If someone is hiding something from his *guru*, and before his *guru* his heart is not open, then how will he be able to go before Bhagavān? This is the very foundation of *śikṣā*, instruction: by honestly serving the *guru* we will learn.

Nārada Ṛṣi observed that, "This Gopa-kumāra is certainly a *viśrambha-sevaka*, and therefore Vaikuṇṭha is not tasteful to him." Therefore Nārada will now start explaining higher *tattva* to him. "Look, here in Vaikuṇṭha everything is *cinmaya*, and here Bhagavān has thousands of forms."

What is the meaning? There are many forms of Varāha, many forms of Mīna, and many forms of Kurma, Nṛsiṁha, Vāmana, Paraśurāma and all other incarnations. It is generally understood that there are twenty-four types of *līlā-avatāras*, but there are not merely twenty-four. There are so many that They cannot possibly be counted. But one incarnation is not different in quality from another incarnation. They are residing in different chambers of Vaikuṇṭha, and all of Them are eternal. Yes, Bhagavān is one, but He appears according to the gradation of the *bhakti* of His devotees. The same one Bhagavān will be seen differently according to the nature of one's *bhakti*.

On the banks of the Yamunā at Kāliya-hrada in Vṛndāvana, a sage named Saubhari Ṛṣi was performing austerities for ten thousand years. But because Garuḍa was coming there and eating fish, Saubhari Ṛṣi became angry and cursed him. Due to this offence, material desire arose within Saubhari Ṛṣi. Next, by his mystic power he assumed fifty forms, married the fifty daughters of Māndhātā Muni, and created fifty palaces with fifty gardens. He arranged them in such a way that they would put Indrapurī to shame with their extensive facility for enjoyment, and he lived like that for the next ten thousand years. His grandchildren and great-grandchildren had all grown up, and one day Māndhātā Muni came there and said, "I have lived without my daughters for so long that now they don't even remember me, and they have no desire whatsoever to come to their father's house. What has happened?" Then he looked around and thought, "There is such opulence here! This is why my daughters have no desire to ever return to visit my home."

These fifty forms that Saubhari Ṛṣi assumed were *kāya-vyūha* forms. When he would lift his hand, all the forms lifted their hand. In *kāya-vyūha* expansions, if the original speaks, then all will speak. If he sleeps, then all will sleep. If he moves, then all will move. One form is real, and the rest are copies. But Bhagavān's incarnations are not like this. All of His forms are independent.

There is one special point concerning the opulence (*aiśvarya*) of Dvārakā, and the sweetness (*mādhurya*) of Vṛndāvana. In Dvārakā, Kṛṣṇa marries sixteen thousand queens. In one palace He is playing dice, somewhere else He is giving cows in charity to a *brāhmaṇa*, somewhere else He is performing a marriage ceremony, in another palace He is performing a fire sacrifice, and in other palaces He is engaged in other activities. All of His forms appear the same as His original form and there is no difference in quality between Them. Here, by *aiśvarya* Kṛṣṇa has manifested into many, many different forms, but all of Them are one in that all are all-powerful and full in all opulences. Each queen is cooking and offering Him preparations, and in one palace He is eating *dahl* and *purī*, in another palace He is eating a rice preparation, in another palace He is eating *sabjī*, in another palace He is eating *pakorās*, and in another palace He is eating sweet-rice. By *aiśvarya*, as the possessor of all potency (*śakti*), in Dvārakā Kṛṣṇa expands into many, many forms, and all the forms are real and independent.

But what happens in Vṛndāvana? It is not a land of *aiśvarya*, opulence. There, over and above opulence is *mādhurya*, sweetness.

How can we understand this clearly? In Vraja there are not just sixteen thousand *gopīs*, but millions; and between every two *gopīs* is one Kṛṣṇa, or between every two Kṛṣṇas is one *gopī*. It appears like this. Here we mustn't even imagine that this is done by *aiśvarya*; it is *mādhurya*. What is the meaning of *mādhurya*? That which is suitable for His pastimes in human form, *nara-līlā*. And that which is opposed to *nara-līlā* is *aiśvarya*. For example, upon seeing the Universal Form of Kṛṣṇa, Arjuna became astonished and said, "By calling You 'friend' I have committed a great offence. In the future I will never again call You 'friend', and never again make You the driver of my chariot. I have committed a great offence." This was *aiśvarya-buddhi*, awareness of Kṛṣṇa's majesty, and was not suitable for *nara-līlā*.

After witnessing Kṛṣṇa's killing of Kaṁsa, Vasudeva and Devakī forgot about lovingly feeding Him milk. This is another type of sentiment that is not suitable for Kṛṣṇa's *nara-līlā*, and therefore it is *aiśvarya*. But in Vṛndāvana, when Kṛṣṇa lifted the massive Govardhana Hill, Yaśodā felt proud and thought, "Today our son lifted Govardhana!" but the feeling that Kṛṣṇa was her son did not leave her. Kṛṣṇa exhibited His opulence of being all-powerful in lifting Govardhana, but the sentiment that Kṛṣṇa was her son never left her heart, and she simply thought, "My son is so strong, there is no one in the entire world stronger than Him!"

In the confusion of divine separation, the *gopīs* were speaking to a bee: "O messenger, we will never have an intimate relationship with Kṛṣṇa. Never at any time, because He is very crooked, a big liar and very deceptive. We will never trust Him, and we will never be able to establish any friendship with Him. Why? He is Bhagavān, isn't He? Paurṇamāsī has told us that He is Bhagavān, and we have faith in that. In His previous birth He was Rāma. He has now appeared with a similar beautiful, dark complexion; that hasn't changed. He is supposed to be a great renunciant and never controlled by a woman. Yet overpowered by a woman, His wife,

He went with her to the jungle. He had all the marks of a *sādhu* and wore the dress of a *sādhu*, and yet went to the jungle with His wife. His wife said, 'Ārya-putra, there is a deer as beautiful as gold; please catch it for me, and then we will take it to Bharata. If You cannot catch it alive, then after killing it with Your arrow, from its skin we will make a beautiful seat suitable for the king's throne. Sitting upon it, Bharata will be greatly pleased, and in the future You will also sit there.'

"Lakṣmaṇa at once said, 'That deer form is the deceptive magic of a demon: please don't go,' but Rāma didn't honour what Lakṣmaṇa said. He claimed that He would never be overpowered by a woman, yet whose words did He honour? His wife's, and He came under her control. That's the kind of person He is. Then another woman came and He cut off her nose and ears! She came begging for *prema* and prepared to give Him everything – was there any fault in that? Rāma appeared to possess all the beauty of the three worlds, so considering the general nature of the female class, there was certainly no fault in her! But what did He do? He cut off her nose and ears. Also, He killed Vāli (the brother of Sugrīva) from a hidden position instead of fighting directly in front of him.

"We have also heard about what He did to Bali Mahārāja. As Vāmanadeva He asked for three steps of land, and Bali was prepared to give it. Then He assumed a massive form and snatched everything. The daughter of Bali said, 'This is not the same form in which You asked for the three steps of land, so we shall not give it to You!' Bali said, 'It's all right, let it be,' but his daughter said to Bhagavān, 'No, I will kill You! I will give You poison and kill You!' and therefore she came later as Pūtanā to do just that. At first, being attracted by His beauty, she had desired to have Him as her son; but upon seeing His cheating ways, she then wanted to kill Him. Could she be blamed? Then Vāmanadeva bound up her father, even after He snatched away everything that came within the measurement of His three steps, just as a crow snatches a fragment of food and then kicks away the basket from which he got it! So we certainly cannot see eye to eye with Kṛṣṇa."

The purport of what they were saying is that they knew that He was Bhagavān because they had faith in what Paurṇamāsī had told them. But in spite of knowing that He was Bhagavān, still His pastimes in human form were the dearest to them, and they became immersed in that loving sentiment. In the confusion of spontaneous love they were saying that they would never be able to have an intimate relationship with Him – this is an example of *mādhurya-bhāva*.

In Vṛndāvana, it appeared that Kṛṣṇa expanded into millions and millions of forms in the *rāsa-līlā*, but actually He didn't assume more forms. Śrīla Viśvanātha Cakravartī Ṭhākura has explained in his commentary on *Śrīmad-Bhāgavatam* that there was only the one original form of Kṛṣṇa, and He danced with such speed and dexterity in the arena of the *rāsa* dance that sometimes He would appear here, sometimes He would appear there, and so each *gopī* thought that "He is dancing with me only." Appearing like a stick that is burning on one end and being waved in a circle, with inconceivable speed and dexterity He was moving amongst them in the circular formation of the *rāsa-līlā*.

We have seen dancing actors in our village near Vārāṇasī who would perform for four or five thousand rupees. One of these dancers would stack pot after pot with plates between them on his head, and on top of everything would be a plate with many candles on it. Dancing in such a way that not even one item would fall, he would move with so much speed it was incredible. So if an ordinary man can dance like this, then how can Kṛṣṇa dance? One and the same Kṛṣṇa was dancing amongst millions of *gopīs* at the same time with inconceivable speed and dexterity. This is *mādhurya*: what is suitable for *nara-līlā*, His human-like pastimes. He assumes separate forms in Dvārakā by *aiśvarya*, but in Vṛndāvana it was not *kāya-vyūha*, incarnations or expansions but the same one Kṛṣṇa moving amongst the *gopīs*, causing each *gopī* to think, "He is dancing with me only."

This *mādhurya* is not present in Vaikuṇṭha, so Gopa-kumāra was not satisfied there. After taking his pulse, Nārada said, "It is a great thing that you desire; therefore I must help you to understand the higher points of *tattva*. For going to Goloka, it is necessary to know all of this."

Chapter Five

Bhagavān's Incarnations are One

Vaikuṇṭha is an expansive land. Included within Vaikuṇṭha are Ayodhyā, Jagannātha Purī, Dvārakā, Mathurā, Vṛndāvana, Govardhana and Rādhā-kuṇḍa. Residing there is not only Kṛṣṇa, but millions and millions of incarnations of Bhagavān. In the four *yugas*, in a *manvantara*, in the two fifty-year segments of Brahmā's life, Bhagavān descends in some form or other. Upon His devotees' attainment of perfection, according to their own specific devotional sentiment they go to live with Him in a particular section of Vaikuṇṭha, taking *darśana* of their favourite Lord and serving Him there.

The sun is reflected in anything that acts as a mirror, but the sun and the reflection are not one. *Bimba* means 'the sun', and *pratibimba* means 'its reflection, which shines in another world'. They are not one, but there is some similarity between them. Unlike the sun, however, there are many, many incarnations of the Lord. Each and every incarnation is directly Bhagavān Himself, and all are eternal, spiritually conscious and blissful (*sac-cid-ānanda*). In Vaikuṇṭha, Bhagavān is not situated in *kāya-vyūha* expansions; instead, in qualitative oneness, He is situated in many different forms for fulfilling the desires of His devotees. In the *Rāmāyaṇa* and other scriptures it is said that Bhagavān is one, and according to the form for which the devotee is praying, He assumes an incarnation as either Nṛsiṁha-avatāra, Kūrma-avatāra, Vāmana-avatāra, Hayagrīva-avatāra – so many incarnations. Bhagavān can come in many forms. Some say that originally Bhagavān has no form, and that when anyone of this world calls Him, then according to that person's particular sentiment, He takes a corresponding form and appears in this world. But this idea is incorrect. All of His forms are real and eternal, and when devotees call Him by the name of a specific form, then in that very form He comes. All the scriptures declare this, and they are fully authoritative due to being completely free of any defect.

There are those who worship Lakṣmīpati Nārāyaṇa with *mantras* such as *oṁ nārāyaṇāya namaḥ* and *oṁ namo bhagavate vāsudevāya*. Dhruva attained perfection through this process. Some chant *oṁ varāhāya namaḥ* to worship Varāha in Navadvīpa-dhāma, some chant *oṁ nṛsiṁhāya namaḥ* or other *mantras* of Nṛsiṁhadeva, and upon attaining perfection those devotees will go to Vaikuṇṭha, but to a special chamber in Vaikuṇṭha. How is Nārāyaṇa situated there? In one place in His Nṛsiṁha form, and in another place in His Varāha form. When there is a necessity in this world for the presence of a particular form, then He comes in that very form. For example, when Kṛṣṇa comes, He comes holding the flute, as Nanda-nandana. He never changes His form. He remains in one form, yet He changes the secondary aspects of His pastimes in a special way. His performing the *rāsa-līlā* with the *gopīs* and playing as a child at the house of Nanda – these pastimes are eternal, but He may change the killing of Kaṁsa. Instead of Kaṁsa it may be Jarāsandha or some other person. According to the necessity of the time the secondary pastimes may be changed, but the eternal *līlās* remain the same.

Those who worship Nārāyaṇa will go to Vaikuṇṭha, but to which chamber in Vaikuṇṭha? To the specific chamber where Lakṣmī and Nārāyaṇa reside. One who chants *japa* of the Nṛsiṁha *mantra* will also go to Vaikuṇṭha, but to a special chamber where there is only worship of Nṛsiṁhadeva. He will never see Rāma or Nārāyaṇa. There are differences in the pastimes of Nṛsiṁha, Varāha and Kūrma, but in *tattva*, They are all non-different.

Before the advent of Vāmanadeva, the demigods worshipped a special four-armed form of Viṣṇu that was established in heaven for their *pūjā*. When a special set of circumstances was created, then in a particular form Vāmanadeva was impelled to come and snatch everything away from Bali Mahārāja. At that time Aditi, the mother of the demigods, had performed some austerities, and because of that He came. Therefore Vāmana performs pastimes that are different from the four-armed Viṣṇu who is always present in heaven, but in *tattva* They are one. Vāmana is a little different from Viṣṇu in that in Vāmana's pastimes there is some deception, and the giving of some special good fortune also. It seemed like robbery, but in it there was so much kindness and *bhakta-vātsalya*, special affection for His devotees. He increased the glories of His devotee. He put Bali Mahārāja into difficulty to make his name immortal for all time. If Vāmana had not come, who would know the name of Bali? For protecting His devotees, He came in a very beautiful form. It seems that He came for protecting the demigods and for cheating the demons, but no; actually He benefited both. In reality Bali Mahārāja received more benefit than the demigods. The demigods got no special benefit, but Bali Mahārāja did. Vāmana snatched the desire for material enjoyment away from Bali and gave him *bhakti*, but He didn't snatch away the demigods' facility for enjoyment; rather He provided it by returning their kingdom to them. So to whom was He more kind? But, like Indra, we desire and pray, "O Lord, please don't snatch our material enjoyment away! Be merciful like this and make our lives plentiful. My son, daughter, money and wife – please don't take them! I will do *bhajana*, and they will remain with me also."

But some pray, "O Lord, You please take all of this away, and give me pure love at Your lotus feet." Which of these is correct? If in both hands there is a *laḍḍū*, will you desire both, or only one? If Bhagavān says, "All right, you take the happiness of material enjoyment, and together with that take pure love for Me also," and

He puts both into our hands, certainly we will take the material enjoyment and not the *bhakti*. However, if we really desire *prema*, then this enjoying spirit must be eradicated. Otherwise there will be cheating and deception in our *bhakti*. But ninety-nine per cent of the people in this world desire like this: "Our material enjoyment must remain intact, our family must remain, our money and palatable food must remain, our business must go on nicely, and together with all of this we will have *bhakti*." So the Lord says, "All right." But He gives them only ordinary *bhakti* to accompany their material enjoyment.

To the demigods Bhagavān gives the responsibility of protecting the world, but the material world is temporary. He says "Do this service for Me" and gives them their posts, but then some of them think, "I have become the master of the three worlds. The Lord has given me this position, and now I am the master of the entire universe." They don't understand that this is actually an obstacle to *bhakti*. So He placed this very allurement in the hands of Indra, and snatched that same allurement away from Bali Mahārāja, giving him pure *bhakti* instead. Many people do not understand that this is a special activity of mercy He performed for Bali.

Assuming an incarnation in this world and performing such beautiful pastimes is something Nārāyaṇa will not do. The four-armed form that is present there in heaven will not do this. Nārāyaṇa will never cheat as Vāmana did. He will also bestow *prema*, but He won't allow Himself to be viewed as a cheater. Vāmana cheated in the vision of ordinary people. He begged for three steps of land, then made His steps very, very large, and stole everything. Vāmana will perform such variegated pastimes and may even be seen as a cheater, but Nārāyaṇa will never do this. So in this way, in the pastimes of Rāma and other incarnations of Bhagavān there is uniqueness. In *tattva* They are all one, but in His pastimes, His special affectionate dealings with His devotees, and His *rasa*, there will be some differences.

In the scriptures it says that there is a final dissolution when the two fifty-year segments of Brahmā's life have passed. Along with Brahmā, nature will merge into Garbhodakaśāyī Viṣṇu. Then He also will disappear and all will merge into Kāraṇodakaśāyī Viṣṇu. So many *jīvas* will merge into the limbs of Viṣṇu at that time, and those that are liberated will go to Vaikuṇṭha with Brahmā. The others will again become embodied and return to this *cakra*, or cycle, of *māyā*. At that time, Mahā-Mīna, the fish incarnation, is to be seen.

After Mārkaṇḍeya Ṛṣi had been performing austerities for a long time, one day he was bathing in the Gaṅgā and a small fish came into his begging bowl (*kamaṇḍalu*). He took it home, and then the fish said, "O sage, I have come into your *kamaṇḍalu*, but there is no space for Me here. Please place Me in a larger body of water."

Then Mārkaṇḍeya looked and saw that really the fish had become larger. So he placed the fish in a small pond, but after some time, the fish came to him in a dream and said, "O sage, now I am so big, I can no longer stay in this pond." So Mārkaṇḍeya lifted the fish out and placed Him in the river, but the fish again enlarged in the river and said, "Here also I cannot stay. Please place Me in the ocean."

By his yogic power Mārkaṇḍeya placed the fish in the ocean. Then he saw in a dream that there was to be a causal dissolution, like the one at the end of Brahmā's day. The final dissolution comes at the end of Brahmā's one hundred years, but this and the one that comes at the end of his day can both be called *nitya-pralaya*.

The fish said, "The water will be rising and I will come to you. You must collect seeds of all the things in the world – vegetable seeds, a mango seed, a mustard seed, everything. Then you must collect two of each species of bird and animal and be ready to attach a strong boat to Me in the morning when I arrive."

During the night Mārkaṇḍeya made the arrangement. He made a strong boat with a rope attached to it, and placed the seeds of all species of life in it. When he was ready, he saw that the entire universe was being flooded with flowing water, and nothing could be seen. The water was slowly rising, and gradually covered all of the high places. The fish had assumed a massive form with two horns, and He said, "Bind the boat to My horns." The sage did so, and Mahā-Mīna took everyone away on the water. This dissolution lasts for one whole night of Brahmā. The sage went without eating or drinking the entire time, and he couldn't find a place to take some rest. Thinking, "What kind of life is this?", he was very unhappy.

Eventually they arrived at Prayaga. There, Mārkaṇḍeya could see only a *banyan* tree and nothing else. At the top of the tree there was only one leaf where Vaṭaśāyī Viṣṇu was sleeping and performing the pastime of sucking His toe. He looked towards the sage very mercifully and consoled him, and transmitted *śakti* into him. He made an arrangement for the sage's sustenance and then said, "In a few days this will all be over and you will again become a progenitor (*prajāpati*), and from Brahmā all creation will again take place."

This is one Mīna-avatāra. This Mīna incarnation resides in Vaikuṇṭha, and when the necessity arises He comes to this world. His *tattva* is non-different from Nārāyaṇa. His pastimes are variegated, but in *tattva* They are one.

Another Mīna incarnation protected the Vedas. The demons had stolen the Vedas and thrown them into the water of the dissolution and the Vedas had disappeared. The tendency of demons is to be greatly destructive, and now also we see that the Vedic scriptures are slowly disappearing. If people don't respect them, what will happen? They will disappear, slowly. The Vedas will not remain, you won't be able to find the *Bhāgavatam*, and such spiritual talks will disappear altogether. The mood of

Vṛndāvana and Mathurā will change, and after some time men will also change. They won't respect holy men and saints, and they won't respect the *Gītā* and the *Bhāgavatam*. Like this, the Vedas had disappeared, and to protect them, another Mīna incarnation appeared.

This Mīna incarnation saved Satyavrata Muni, who had at that time offered a prayer known as the *Dāmodarāṣṭaka*. Taking so many things with him, he stayed in the ocean for a long time, and the Vedas and scriptures were kept in his heart. Again the dissolution was finished, and again in the four directions creation took place. So there is not just one Mīna incarnation, but many. In Vaikuṇṭha also, there are different chambers suitable for Their particular devotees, and Satyavrata Muni's worshipful Lord is this particular Mīna incarnation.

There is also the Kūrma incarnation. At the time of churning the ocean of milk, the demons and demigods came together and agreed that everything produced from the churning would be distributed. Viṣṇu, through the medium of Brahmā, gave them some advice; otherwise nothing would have been produced. They placed the Mandara Mountain in the middle of the ocean, but there was no foundation for it, so the mountain immediately sank. They thought, "This will be very difficult. How will we remove it from the ocean? How will we find a foundation upon which to churn?"

So they worshipped Viṣṇu, and He came in the form of a tortoise, Kūrma. "For your good fortune, I will accept the form of a tortoise. Place the mountain on Me, wind the snake Vāsuki around it, and then churn."

They placed the mountain on Kūrma, and wrapped the king of snakes Vāsuki around it. In one direction was the mouth of Vāsuki and in the other direction was his tail. The demigods said to the demons, "Since we are senior to you, we will take the direction of the head. We are worthy of more respect than you."

The demons replied, "No, we will not give you this respect! We will take the direction of the head. The tail is inferior; we will not take it!" So the demons demanded the head side, not understanding the trickery of the demigods. But the demigods insisted, "You are our little brothers, the sons of Diti. Therefore, whatever is produced by the churning, we will take first and you will take the remainder. And since we are senior to you, we will take the direction of Vāsuki's head."

But the demons were adamant. "No, it can never be like that! We are superior! What is this, that we are younger? We are superior, we will take the direction of the head."

The demigods actually wanted to take the tail end, because they knew that in the midst of the churning, during the hissing of the snake, deadly poison would be emitted from his mouth. But the demons didn't know this. They quickly grabbed the mouth end, and while making a great effort to churn, it became very hot, poison was produced from the snake, and they were burnt. They thought, "The demigods have tricked us! All right; next time we will understand. We will do exactly the opposite of what they say."

As they churned the ocean of milk, first poison was produced, then Lakṣmī came out, then nectar was produced, Dhanvantari came out, the white elephant of the demigods was produced, a horse was produced, and many other wonderful things. When Lakṣmī-devī appeared, she looked all around and wondered, "Who will I marry?" She began considering, and felt that everyone she saw was full of faults. She saw everyone – even Brahmā – and she rejected them all. Finally Viṣṇu came there, and she put the garland around His neck and married Him.

While the churning was going on, Kūrma had an itching sensation on His back, and the churning movement of the massive mountain scratched His itch. At that time, His breathing in and out created the low and high tides of the ocean. Some say the influence of the moon is the cause of this, but the cause given in the scriptures is correct.

Another Kūrma incarnation appeared in another *yuga* or *manvantara* to support the Earth planet throughout its entire duration. These are two separate Kūrma incarnations.

Regarding Varāhadeva, before the creation there was only water. Brahmā heard a sound indicating that he should perform *tapasya*, austerities. After this he met Nārāyaṇa and heard the four root verses (*catuḥ-ślokī*) of the *Bhāgavatam*, and was empowered to create. But for creation there must be a foundation, and at that time there was no base because the Earth was submerged in water. So Varāha, in the form of a very, very small entity like a weevil, emerged from Brahmā's nose and immediately doubled in size. Then when He was a little distance away, He assumed a form so large that He filled the entire sky, and He jumped straight into the ocean with both His snout and His feet pointed downward. Such violent waves were produced that they even reached up to heaven and Brahmaloka, and water was spread in all directions. When Varāhadeva arrived at Rasātala, He took the Earth on His snout and established it above the water. This is one Varāha incarnation.

There is also another Varāha incarnation who found that when He went to Rasātala, Hiraṇyākṣa was there waiting for Him. Hiraṇyākṣa had been searching for his equal in heroics, and he had asked Nārada where he could find such a person. He was told to go to Varuṇadeva, who told him, "Yes, you will find a suitable opponent, and He will grind you to pieces."

"Who is this person?"

"Viṣṇu."

"Where can I find Him?"

"He is everywhere, but finding Him is very, very difficult. When you meet Him, He will destroy your pride."

Hiraṇyākṣa was told that if he went to Rasātala at the time of the final dissolution, he would meet Viṣṇu there. He arrived there first, and he remained waiting there for a very long time submerged in the water. Finally Varāha arrived there and took the Earth on His snout, just as a huge elephant holds a small flower or as someone holds a mustard seed; it was so easy for Him. He established the Earth above the water, and then turned to fight with the demon. They fought for thousands of years, and in the end Varāha killed Hiraṇyākṣa with His club, thereby destroying his pride. Then He disappeared. These are two separate Varāha incarnations. One is white, the other is black.

Another incarnation is Yajṣa-Varāha. In each of His pores are millions of *brahmāṇḍas*, and He accepts the results of sacrifice. By His mercy the Earth heard the Purāṇas – the same ones written by Vyāsa – so from this we can understand that the Purāṇas are eternal. Devotees prayed to this Varāha because the Earth's surface was too rough and they were unable to do any farming. It would not retain water, and the people could not live without grains and water. So being merciful, Varāha incarnated and with His teeth He uprooted big mountains and made the Earth's surface smooth. This is the nature of a boar, that with his snout he digs. Afterwards the Earth appeared as if it had been ploughed.

At that time, the Earth personified assumed the form of a female boar. Her name was Dharitrī-devī, and she was the potency (*śakti*) of Bhū-devī. Viṣṇu assumed the form of a boar, so she became a female boar, and from them Narakāsura was born. Originally his name was Dharitrī-nandana, not Narakāsura, but as a result of falling into bad association he became a demon.

Association is what makes *bhakti* appear in any heart, and also that which can make it disappear. It is the cause of our bondage or liberation. We will become just like those with whom we keep company, so bad association is the most dangerous enemy of our hearts. By keeping bad company even the son of Bhagavān and the Earth personified became sinful. Whose company did he keep? Duryodhana, Śakuni, Kaṁsa, Jarāsandha – so many personalities who were opposed to Kṛṣṇa – and all were atheistic. He took the association of all these people and then tried to give Bhagavān trouble. Therefore he became known as Narakāsura.

All together there are five Varāha incarnations mentioned in the scriptures. They all reside in Vaikuṇṭha, and when there is a necessity for one of Them in this world, He comes and gives *darśana* to His devotees in that very form. After those devotees attain perfection, they go to Vaikuṇṭha to serve Him directly there as well.

There are different incarnations of Nṛsiṁhadeva as well. One incarnation killed Hiraṇyakaśipu and protected Prahlāda. Another is *mātṛcakra-pramatta*. *Mātṛcakra* means those women who were detrimental to the welfare of the world. When their power increased, Nṛsiṁha Bhagavān appeared to subdue them. Another incarnation came in the form of a cat and performed many different pastimes; He also subdued demons and protected devotees.

In South India, there is one deity called Jiyara-Nṛsiṁha and another called Pānā-Nṛsiṁha. They are separate incarnations. They appeared in different *kalpas*, and there are differences in Their pastimes. There was once a wild boar in a kingdom where in all directions there were mountains and jungle. In that place was a farmer who was a great devotee. He was growing corn, and every day this boar came and ate it and destroyed his crop. He was upset that his field was being destroyed, so he constructed a platform in the middle of the field. He thought that he would sit there during the night and watch for that boar. That night the boar came and broke everything again, so taking a stick, the farmer got down from the platform and chased it. The boar ran with the farmer following behind and after a little while, laughing, the boar stopped and stood, displaying the form of Nṛsiṁha. "For the purpose of mercifully giving you My *darśana*, I have done this. Now you can offer corn to Me. It is My favourite food, and I will fulfil all the desires of your heart. Get money from the king and establish Me on top of that mountain where only *campā* flowers grow."

He was Nṛsiṁha, but He assumed the form of a boar. On the day of *akṣaya-tṛtīyā* the *pujārīs* apply sandalwood paste to that deity and He reveals His form as a boar. That's all – only on one day of the year He gives that *darśana*. This is Jiyara-Nṛsiṁha, and He appeared in one particular *kalpa*. Therefore in some places devotees worship a combined form of Nṛsiṁha and Varāha.

In this way, Hayagrīva, Haṁsa – in the scriptures you will find two, four or five of each incarnation, but Their *tattva* is one. According to the sentiments of Their devotees, and for receiving different types of service from them, They are all eternally residing in Vaikuṇṭha.

Speaking to Gopa-kumāra in Vaikuṇṭha, Nārada is saying, "Here people are performing *pūjā* of Paraśurāma, of Nṛsiṁha, of Vāmana, of many incarnations. If a devotee comes here and worships a particular deity, and then after some time leaves that *pūjā* to worship another deity, there is no fault in it. In your lifetime you have worshipped many incarnations of Bhagavān. Therefore according to one's own *niṣṭhā* he can go here or there, because Bhagavān is one. I am telling you this because I can see that you do not like it here. Even while residing in Vaikuṇṭha, if your internal *svarūpa* is that of a cowherd boy, then you will always desire to worship Gopāla. Therefore you are not happy here, but there is no fault in this. This is a very deep thing; it is not written anywhere, but taking your pulse, I have ascertained the reason for your dissatisfaction. Here, will Lakṣmī-devī allow anyone else to massage the feet of her Lord? Will she allow anyone to serve Him food? She won't. She thinks, 'It is my duty alone.' You can only stand at a distance and offer prayers to Him. If some devotee comes here and tries to sit on the lap of Nārāyaṇa, as Prahlāda sits on the lap of Nṛsiṁha, she won't allow it.

"From here you should continue your journey, and you will experience more variegated pastimes and more intimate *rasa*. I have explained all of this to you so that first you will understand that all incarnations of Bhagavān are one in *tattva*. Therefore there is no fault in leaving one incarnation to go to another because They are all one and the same. They only appear different to accommodate the various sentiments of Their devotees."

Chapter Six

Kṛṣṇa's Glories are Inconceivable

All of the incarnations of Bhagavān are the same in quality, just as from one candle we can light ten candles and all will be the same in quality. Which one is the original and which ones were lit from that, we can't tell.

etac ca vṛndā-vipine 'gha-hantur
hṛtvārbha-vatsān anubhūtam asti
śrī-brahmaṇā dvāravatī-pure ca
prasāda-vargeṣu mayā bhramitvā

Bṛhad-bhāgavatāmṛta (2.4.164)

Nārada is saying, "When Brahmā stole the boys and calves in Vṛndāvana, he experienced how Śrī Kṛṣṇa, the killer of the Agha demon, is one and yet expands into many, and I myself experienced it when I visited His palaces in Dvārakā."

In Vṛndāvana, the mothers and fathers of the *gopīs* and *gopas*, upon seeing the beauty and sweetness of Kṛṣṇa – His speech, His behaviour, all of His charming sweetness – the desire comes in them that He be their son. At the time when the cows are giving milk to their calves, they think, "Sometimes Kṛṣṇa comes and drinks our milk with His own mouth. We desire that He be our calf so we can feed Him milk." In Vraja-maṇḍala there are so many cows, mothers, and mothers who already have sons, and they all desire that Kṛṣṇa become their son so they can feed Him milk and show Him motherly affection. Not so much when Kṛṣṇa enters their houses, steals milk and drinks it, but in the late afternoon when Kṛṣṇa returns from taking the cows out to graze. At that time, Mother Yaśodā gives Him motherly affection and wipes His face, and all the mothers and cows desire very strongly in their hearts that Kṛṣṇa be their son. Leaving their own children, all the mothers come first to look after Kṛṣṇa. Then they return to their own children, take them in their laps, wipe their faces and give them all affection.

Kṛṣṇa knows their desire. How does He know? It says in one verse of *Śrīmad-Bhāgavatam* that when Kṛṣṇa is playing with the *gopīs* and is fully absorbed in performing pastimes, He forgets everything: "Where am I?" Any loss or gain for Himself in this activity, any loss or gain for the world – all of this is forgotten. At this time, if some enemy attacks, what will happen? A demon like Aghāsura or Bakāsura may come, but everything will be forgotten. All household duties, eating, drinking, bathing – all is forgotten. He is so absorbed in relishing the *prema* of the *gopīs* that all is forgotten and He is aware of nothing else. The affection of His mothers, the affection of His friends – all is forgotten.

Regarding that time, Viśvanātha Cakravartī Ṭhākura asks a question. "You devotees are praying, 'O Kṛṣṇacandra, give me the *darśana* of Your lotus feet,' and you are crying and crying, but who will hear this prayer? Kṛṣṇa has already forgotten everything! When Kṛṣṇa has forgotten everything, then *sarvajñatā*, His quality of knowing what is in everyone's heart, is diminished. That is an aspect of *aiśvarya*, one of His opulences. At that time when He is supremely absorbed – sometimes falling at the feet of the *gopīs*, trying to appease them, serving them and receiving service from them – He is so absorbed in this that He forgets all other things of the world. All *sarvajñatā* has been abandoned, and all six kinds of opulence have been forgotten. Then who will hear your prayer?

"Knowing everything is a quality of *aiśvarya*, so if it comes at this time, the mood of *mādhurya* will be disturbed. So who will come to hear this prayer? This is a big problem. We are praying, and that is meaningless? If there is no listener, certainly it will be meaningless. Paramātmā is Kṛṣṇa's expansion; He exists everywhere as the all-pervading witness. Will He know? But if we are praying directly to Govinda and only Paramātmā is aware of it, what is the use? We are praying to the king and the doorman is listening – what will be the benefit in that? We won't be satisfied with that. So what then? Will our prayer not go directly to Kṛṣṇa? If our prayer doesn't reach Kṛṣṇa's ears, then it is as if we are crying and no one can hear. And if no one hears, then who will do something to relieve that crying? If a small baby is crying for milk and no one hears him, what will he do? Our crying will merely be the same. But don't worry, don't be disturbed; Kṛṣṇa will hear."

We may think, "But how? If He listens, it will be *aiśvarya*." To resolve this, Kṛṣṇa possesses two qualities: He is simultaneously *mugdha* and *sarvajña*. What is the meaning of *mugdha*? Becoming so spellbound in love that it is just as if He doesn't know anything. Yaśodā grabs His ear and says, "You go to the corner and continuously sit down and stand again! Don't You steal anymore!" And He will really do it! Taking a small stick Yaśodā will say, "Today You will not get away without a beating!" And Kṛṣṇa will say, "Mother! Don't hit Me!" with tears coming from His eyes. This is called *mugdhatā*, being spellbound in emotion. Fear itself is afraid of Him, yet He becomes frightened when Mother Yaśodā approaches Him with a stick. She will not beat Him; she just says that she will – but He cries and the tears are flowing. Here, is Kṛṣṇa really crying, or is He just making a show of it? Ordinary people will say, "Will Bhagavān cry? He won't cry. What could He possibly be afraid of?" But *premī* devotees will say that He is really crying, and this is called *mugdhatā*.

If Jarāsandha, Pūtanā, Aghāsura, Bakāsura, Kaṁsa or Narakāsura come, then this young boy named Kṛṣṇa kills them. This is His quality of *sarva-śaktimattā*, having all power. He is as well known for this as He is for knowing everything, yet at the same time He becomes spellbound in *līlā*. For example, once, Kṛṣṇa called for Uddhava: "Uddhava, come over here. Today we have a serious problem."

"What is it?"

"Today, from Hastināpura, an invitation to the *rājasūya-yajña* has come, and tomorrow it will commence there. In the opposite direction, Jarāsandha is causing a great disturbance and it is necessary to kill him. We should do both things, but I can't understand how. You are a clever, intelligent man, My minister and friend; tell Me, what should I do? Should we go now to the Pāṇḍavas' *rājasūya-yajña*, or should we go and kill Jarāsandha?"

Uddhava thought, "Look at this! Svayam Bhagavān, who knows all and has all powers, is asking me? And it seems that He is really asking, not that He is just giving Me respect. It seems that He is not just playing the part of a king, and that He is not just observing the formality of taking advice from a minister. Is Kṛṣṇa really just observing this formality, or is He sincerely asking? It seems from looking at His face that He is sincerely asking me!"

Then Uddhava replied, "O Lord, according to my consideration, it will be good if we go now to the *rājasūya-yajña* in Hastināpura. We can accomplish both objectives with one action. For completion of the sacrifice, a horse will be sent off so that any king who wants to present a challenge may do so, and You and Arjuna can follow behind it. Please take Bhīma also. Eventually that horse will arrive in the Māgadha province of Jarāsandha and You can kill him there. Then the *rājasūya-yajña* will be completed, and You can kill Jarāsandha also."

Kṛṣṇa patted Uddhava on the back. He was very, very pleased. He could not make the decision Himself, and when His prime minister gave such wise advice, He was very pleased.

So Bhagavān is both *mugdha* and *sarvajña* at the same time. This is not a fault, but rather by His inconceivable potency it is one of His qualities. It is stated in the *Vedānta-sutra* that all contradictory qualities are completely harmonised in Kṛṣṇa: *viruddha-dharmaṁ tasmin na citram.* In Kṛṣṇa both *mugdhatā* and *sarvajñatā* are going on together, and there is no fault in this. This is not possible for anyone else. If any human being says that they possess this quality, they are only a fraud.

Kṛṣṇa is *sarvajña* like this: when the *rāsa-līlā* starts, Kṛṣṇa sees so many *gopīs*, and they are all desiring that "Kṛṣṇa will be with me only, He will appease me, and I will be the most fortunate." Kṛṣṇa knows this, and He dances in such a way that it appears that between every two *gopīs* is one Kṛṣṇa, and He fulfils their desires. This is *sarvajñatā*. Such *sarvajñatā* is not seen even in Rāma or Nārāyaṇa. Along with this, when Śrīmatī Rādhikā disappears from the *rāsa* dance, Kṛṣṇa thinks, "Where has She gone?" He doesn't know. He is *sarvajña*, but still He becomes upset and cries for Her. Just as Rāmacandra really cries for Sītā-devī, here Kṛṣṇa is really crying for Rādhikā. And when They reunite? He becomes Hers only. She says, "Today You decorate My hair," and taking a flower He follows behind Her. She says, "I am unable to walk any further," and He takes Her on His shoulders. All of these things are *mugdhatā*. This is the very pinnacle of both *rāsa* and *bhagavattā*, Bhagavān's nature as the Supreme.

Regarding the older *gopīs*, they all desired that Kṛṣṇa would become their son, and all of the cows desired that Kṛṣṇa would become their calf. Kṛṣṇa saw that drinking the milk of one mother would not fill His stomach. The love of one mother would not be sufficient. Similarly, the love of one *gopī* is not sufficient for Him. For Him, millions of *gopīs* are necessary. He desires the affection of millions of mothers, and that will fill His "stomach". Therefore, one day He thought, "Today in Vraja, I will have millions of mothers, I will marry millions of *gopīs*, and I will become the calf of millions of cows. Let's see, how will I do it? By connection with the Supersoul it could be done, but in this human-like form, in *nara-līlā*, it will be very difficult."

For this purpose He bewildered Brahmā. He sent inspiration into the heart of Brahmā to come there to Vraja. Then Brahmā saw the killing of Aghāsura and thought, "This is a marvellous thing! How did this young cowherd boy give liberation to that demon?"

To see more pastimes of Kṛṣṇa, Brahmā could have prayed like this: "O Lord, I want to see more of Your *līlā*. Please be merciful to me and show me more pastimes." It is an ordinary prayer, and Kṛṣṇa would have fulfilled it, but Brahmā didn't do this. He thought, "All right; I will see more of His activities for myself."

One way to find out what you want to know is to ask someone. Another way is to just sit patiently and wait for someone to automatically tell you. Leaving aside the desire to know, one may think, "If I am qualified to understand, then he will tell me." But instead, in order to find out something for himself, Brahmā thought, "I will place an obstacle in His way." How did this idea come into his mind? In the form of *caitya-guru* Bhagavān causes something to arise in someone's heart. He Himself inspired this idea within Brahmā so Brahmā would place an obstacle in His *līlā*, and then Kṛṣṇa would be able to fulfil all of His objectives yet still remain within *nara-līlā*, His human-like pastimes.

Therefore, in the afternoon of the same day He gave liberation to Aghāsura, Kṛṣṇa was with the other cowherd boys. They were very hungry, so they all sat down to eat. With great eagerness and great love, while laughing and playing and amusing one another, they were eating. Brahmā observed this and thought, "This is the right time." The calves had continued moving on. By the influence of Yogamāyā they had seen some especially green grass for grazing, so they went further and further ahead until they were very far away. Meanwhile, the *sakhās* were still eating, and when the calves were beyond the eyesight of everyone, Brahmā stole them. Some say that he took them to his own Brahmaloka, and some say that he hid them in the caves of Govardhana. Govardhana is quite extensive and there are many caves there.

When they didn't see the calves, the boys said, "Where have the calves gone?" Kṛṣṇa suggested, "I will go and bring them back Myself. I will just play the flute and they will return of their own accord. You all just continue eating; I am going."

Why did Kṛṣṇa do this? To play a trick on Brahmā, and so that He could become the boys and calves Himself. Therefore He arranged precisely what Brahmā desired – that He would somehow become separated from the other boys. Brahmā saw this and thought, "The very thing I desired has now happened! I wanted to kidnap the boys when Kṛṣṇa was not watching, and now I have the perfect opportunity! Of His own accord Kṛṣṇa has gone away."

Kṛṣṇa went away, and how did He go? In the carefree manner of a young cowherd, with a handful of yoghurt and rice. But searching and searching, He thought, "Where have the calves gone?" This is also *mugdhatā*.

After a little while, when He couldn't find the calves, He returned to the lunch area and saw that the boys had also vanished. Brahmā had also taken them and confined them within a cave. Kṛṣṇa actually didn't know anything. Searching and searching, He couldn't see His friends, and the calves were nowhere to be found. He still had that uneaten rice in His hand, and His face became withered from unhappiness. He became overwhelmed with fear, thinking, "What will I say to all of their mothers? All the calves have been lost, and now I do not see the boys either. What will I tell all of the mothers and Vrajavāsīs?" Kṛṣṇa was very worried. His limbs were covered with dust, and His face was withered from hunger, thirst and unhappiness. *Sarvajñatā* was absent here.

After a little while, Yogamāyā thought, "I should offer some service." She suddenly appeared there to render service, and then

Kṛṣṇa remembered, "Oh yes, through Yogamāyā I engineered this entire situation to create this pastime and to fulfil the desires of the Vrajavāsīs."

Then Kṛṣṇa expanded and assumed forms identical to those of the boys and calves. He sat His friends back down and fed them Himself, and everyone was very happy. Their eating, drinking and laughing went on as it had before, and then in the late afternoon they all returned to their homes. All the mothers thought, "Ahh, my son has returned!" Previously they had gone first to Kṛṣṇa to look after Him and give Him motherly affection, and then attended to their own children. But that day they all looked after their own children first, and forgot about Kṛṣṇa. Only Yaśodā looked after Kṛṣṇa, and the rest of the mothers looked after their own children. That day the cows disregarded their younger calves, and showed more attention to the older calves who had returned from the forest with Kṛṣṇa, feeding them milk and licking them. For one year the *līlā* went on like this.

Then Baladeva Prabhu thought, "What is this? The calves have come running from Govardhana, and the cows are showing affection first to the older ones, not caring for the younger ones? Why is this? And the mothers who used to attend to Kṛṣṇa first are now tending their own children first. Why? What has happened? Why is it like this?" Because Kṛṣṇa had become those children and calves Himself, He received much more affection. All of the mothers and cows had their desire to have Kṛṣṇa as their son or calf fulfilled, and He received the affection that He desired from millions of mothers. Also in that very year He married millions of *kiśorīs*. Through all those boys that He became, He married all the young girls of Vṛndāvana, so all of His objectives were accomplished.

Now that everything was completed, Kṛṣṇa sent some internal inspiration to Baladeva to bring this pastime to a close. Otherwise Baladeva wouldn't have known anything of it. Baladeva said, "My dear brother, I don't understand. Whose illusory potency is this? Is it the illusory energy of the demigods, or Mahāmāyā, or someone else? This is not My illusory potency, and if it were the illusory potency of the demigods or Mahāmāyā, then I would understand." Then He thought, "Oh, Kṛṣṇa Himself has become all of these boys and calves? Why has He done it?" He asked Kṛṣṇa, "My dear brother, what is this? Until today I didn't understand, but today I see something unique. Why have You become so many boys and calves also? What is this?" Kṛṣṇa smiled. To fulfil the desires of so many people and to bewilder Brahmā, through the medium of His own Yogamāyā potency He engineered this pastime.

After a little while, Brahmā came from his own abode, worried. He had found that there was no place for him in his own planet. Kṛṣṇa had also assumed the form of Hiraṇyagarbha Brahmā and had gone to Brahmaloka. There He told the doorman, "If someone taking my form as Brahmā comes here, don't allow him to enter."

When Brahmā returned to his abode after stealing the boys and calves, six months passed. It was only one minute for him, but his one minute is six months for us. He arrived at his Brahmaloka and the doorman asked him, "Who are you? Our grandfather Brahmā is here, and he has said that if any other four-headed Brahmā comes here, he is not allowed to enter. You cannot enter; stay outside! You must be a creation of *māyā*." Brahmā thought, "Oh! Kṛṣṇa Himself has come here? I have committed an offence at His feet; I must return to Earth immediately." In coming back to Vraja, another six months elapsed. Altogether one Earth year had passed.

etac ca vṛndā-vipine 'gha-hantur
hṛtvārbha-vatsān anubhūtam asti

Bṛhad-bhāgavatāmṛta (2.4.164)

After stealing the cowherd boys and calves, Brahmājī experienced how Kṛṣṇa is simultaneously one and millions. *Eko bahu syām*: Kṛṣṇa is one and becomes many, yet becoming many still remains one. First Brahmā saw, "Here Kṛṣṇa is sitting with rice in His hand and eating, just as He was that day one year ago, and with Him are so many boys and calves. Are they the same ones that I stole, or are they different ones? It is possible that by His own *māyā* Kṛṣṇa has taken them from the caves. Who are they? Which are the real ones?"

To see about this, he went to Govardhana Hill. He saw that the boys and calves were just as he had left them, sleeping in *yoganidrā*. Then returning to Kṛṣṇa, he saw that the boys and calves were there also. He thought, "When I come here, Kṛṣṇa brings the boys and calves here, and when I go to Govardhana, He places them back there."

Therefore, with two of his faces and four of his eyes, he looked in the direction of the cave, and at the same time with the other two faces and four eyes he looked over to where Kṛṣṇa was. He saw that the boys and calves were sleeping in the cave, and simultaneously they were eating and drinking with Kṛṣṇa, performing pastimes. Then suddenly he saw that the entire scene had disappeared, and that all of the boys and calves with Kṛṣṇa had assumed the forms of four-armed Nārāyaṇa. In addition, he saw how the human beings, Brahmās, Śaṅkaras, demigods, animals, plants and so on of each and every *brahmāṇḍa* were all offering prayers to these four-armed Nārāyaṇas and performing *kīrtana*.

Brahmā saw that each of the four-armed forms had all of the qualities of the original: all were *sac-cid-ānanda*, all were full of the six opulences, all were fully omniscient, and all had the sixty qualities of Bhagavān. Only Kṛṣṇa Himself has four more. The boys had so many blankets, sticks, flutes, horns and other things, and they also assumed four-armed forms. Witnessing this, Brahmā became very astonished and began offering prayers. "O Bhagavān, first You showed that You were alone, then You showed that all of the boys and calves are all Bhagavān, and finally You showed that everything is Bhagavān. Without Bhagavān, nothing can have its existence. No *jīva* can exist, and no material object can exist, but at the same time everything is not directly Bhagavān. But I have seen that all of the boys and calves are You only. All have the qualities of Bhagavān; it is not that some forms are inferior or superior. After this I looked again, and all of these forms had disappeared, and only You, Kṛṣṇa, remained."

After witnessing this pastime, Brahmā said, "O Bhagavān, who can describe the glories of Your inconceivable potency (*acintya-śakti*)?"

jānanta eva jānantu
kiṁ bahūktyā na me prabho
manaso vapuṣo vāco
vaibhavaṁ tava go-caraḥ

Śrīmad-Bhāgavatam (10.14.38)

Those people who say that they know Bhagavān, that they know the glories of Bhagavān – in reality they know nothing. Until today I also thought like that, but actually I am unable to describe His glories.

What to speak of Brahmā, even Kṛṣṇa Himself cannot describe His own glories. He cannot find the depth of the glories of His own name, qualities and form. Assuming the complexion and sentiment of Śrīmatī Rādhikā, He became Śrī Caitanya Mahāprabhu. He descended in this form to investigate His own glories, but He still couldn't find their depth. In this way Kṛṣṇa is inconceivable. He is one, but becomes many. He is *mugdha*, and simultaneously He is *sarvajña*. All contradictory qualities are harmonised in Him. Don't attempt to understand this through mental speculation! Only if one is completely surrendered to Him can one know a little of His glories. Think only of serving Him. Trying to count or measure His glories will only be troublesome. Therefore Brahmā said, "I cannot find the depth of Your inconceivable glories." The glories of Bhagavān are limitless. Who can find the depth of them? Brahmā couldn't, Baladeva Prabhu couldn't, even Kṛṣṇa Himself couldn't. Therefore don't try to fathom the glories of Bhagavān through logic and debate. By rendering service to Him we will obtain some understanding of His glories. Therefore we should make an effort only for *bhakti*.

Another reason that Kṛṣṇa showed this pastime was for the bewilderment of Brahmā. In the midst of his life Brahmā was sometimes in illusion. Thinking himself to be the master of the entire universe, once Brahmā went to Dvārakāpurī to meet with Kṛṣṇa. Arriving at the gates, he said to the doorman, "I have come to see Kṛṣṇa."

The doorman went to Kṛṣṇa and said, "Someone named Brahmā has come to see You."

Kṛṣṇa said, "Go and ask him 'Which Brahmā?' "

The doorman returned and asked, "Which Brahmā are you?"

He replied, "I am four-headed Brahmā, the grandfather of all!"

The doorman went to Kṛṣṇa and repeated exactly what Brahmā had said. Kṛṣṇa smiled and thought, "I have given him this post, and just see how he has become proud." So Kṛṣṇa said, "Go and call him."

Brahmā entered the Sudharmā assembly hall. In that place even if millions and millions of people entered, there would still be space for them. It could become very extensive, and it could also become very small. On hot days it would become cool, and on cold days it would be warm. Just as one desired, it would become. When Brahmā entered, he saw this vast royal assembly hall, and Kṛṣṇa was seated in the middle. There were millions of other Brahmās present there. The smallest of them, an eight-headed Brahmā, was seated in the back. In the front there were Brahmās with thousands of heads. Their crowns were composed entirely of jewels, and when they were getting up from offering obeisances, the sound of the crowns clanging together resounded in the four directions. He saw other Brahmās with sixteen heads, others with sixty-four heads, and all of them were much, much larger than himself. His pride now destroyed, he went and offered his prostrated obeisances to Kṛṣṇa. Getting up, he saw that everything had disappeared and only Kṛṣṇa was left, smiling. Such are His glories – unlimited. And for one who has gone to Vaikuṇṭha as Gopa-kumāra has, he will see that the glories of not just one but of all the incarnations are like this.

Chapter Seven

Bhagavān's Inconceivable Potency

When Brahmā stole the *gopas* and calves and Kṛṣṇa Himself became all of them, He took on the same nature as all the boys and calves. He also became the sticks, blankets, everything – all were Kṛṣṇa Himself, and none were different from Him. Brahmā personally experienced this:

durvitarkyā hi sā śaktir
adbhutā parameśvarī
kintv asyaikānta-bhakteṣu
gūḍham kiñcin na tiṣṭhati

Bṛhad-bhāgavatāmṛta (2.4.165)

> Although Bhagavān's potency is wonderful and inconceivable, it is not a secret to His exclusive devotees.

But devotees do not keep the same feelings for all of those *mūrtis*. If they do, then their sentiment will not be perfected. If we see Them all as equal, then will we treat those sticks which Kṛṣṇa became the same as the original form of Kṛṣṇa Himself? Rāmacandra, Nārāyaṇa, Nṛsiṁha, Vāmana – Kṛṣṇa is one with all of Them. So an ordinary man, a neutral person, will consider Them all equal, just as one may consider that all *tulasī* leaves are equal: which one is smaller or bigger, which one has holes in it, which are dry, wet, or immature doesn't matter; all are equal. Similarly, those who are neutral say, "For us, all Vaiṣṇavas are equal. We don't consider who is an *uttama-bhāgavata*, *madhyama-bhāgavata* or *kaniṣṭha*. We see only that they are all Vaiṣṇavas. They all wear saffron cloth, apply *tilaka* and take *harināma*, so for us they are all representatives of Bhagavān."

Some people speak like this, but in *bhagavad-bhakti*, such neutrality is not desirable. In *bhakti* there should be exclusive feeling for one *mūrti*. Kṛṣṇa, Rāma, Nṛsiṁha, Nārāyaṇa – They are all one, but for a devotee one favourite deity (*iṣṭadeva*) must come. Then there can be perfection in *bhajana*. Otherwise, the vision that all are equal and that all are one from the viewpoint of *tattva* is correct, but from the viewpoint of worship (*upāsanā*), there are some shortcomings in it.

For instance, Kṛṣṇa steals from houses and tells lies. Yaśodā asks, "Hey! Have You been stealing from others' houses?"

Kṛṣṇa replies, "When could I have done it? Early in the morning you sent Me to the forest to take the cows grazing. All day they are grazing, and then I bring them back in the early evening. Then I come to you. Tell Me, when could I have stolen anything?"

And He had done it, too! This is *mugdhatā*. This is a positive quality of Bhagavān, which is accepted by devotees, but monists (*nirviśeṣavādīs*) consider this to be a fault. They consider this to be defect and will not understand it. This is a quality of Bhagavān's variegatedness, but a neutral person will not be able to understand it.

In the realm of *bhakti*, neutrality is the most undesirable thing. Exclusive sentiment is the specific quality of *bhakti*; therefore in relation to Kṛṣṇa there will never be neutrality. There is neutrality in Brahman, so this is a desirable quality for *brahmavādīs*, impersonalists. If someone says that complete neutrality is a quality of Kṛṣṇa, then he is certainly a neutral person. In the war between the Pāṇḍavas and the Kauravas, by cleverness and cheating Kṛṣṇa took the side of the Pāṇḍavas, His devotees. One can also say that the sun is neutral. When you are in front of it, it gives you light and heat, but when you remain inside the house you don't get its rays. Then where is the sun's neutrality? The Lord is just like this.

Kṛṣṇa is just seated quietly, just like the master of a house is seated. For everything He has appointed a department head and has told everyone, "All of you do your own work!" Then He just sits quietly and oversees them all. Like this Kṛṣṇa possesses all transcendental potencies (*śaktis*), and lets everyone automatically do their work. In the management of the universe these *śaktis* see to it that there is never any disturbance. There never has been, and never will be; such is the efficacy of His *śaktis*.

Kṛṣṇa stole something, and when the news of His theft reached Yaśodā, she became angry. Parabrahma, the Supreme Being, had stolen from houses and broken pots, so He will have to be punished. But because His limbs are so soft, she will not hit Him, but bind Him; then He will learn His lesson. Taking a rope in her hands, she tried to bind Kṛṣṇa, but the rope was short by a measurement of two fingers' length. She tried again with more rope, and again the rope was two fingers' length short. Trying and trying, from early until ten o'clock in the morning, the rope was still two fingers' length short. At that time, Yaśodā was very astonished, and the *gopīs* were very delighted. Originally they had angrily come to speak against Kṛṣṇa so that He would be given punishment, and now they were clapping their hands and laughing, saying to Yaśodā, "Just see, you cannot control Him! How will you possibly bind Him?" They brought all the ropes of Vraja and still couldn't bind Him. It was always two fingers' length short. Yaśodā had applied such a long rope, and neither His waist or waist ornaments had increased in size, so how is this?

Bhagavān's *acintya-śakti* remains in an inactive state, not doing anything, but is always searching for an opportunity for service. Just like the person who doesn't work all of the time but simply waits for the order of his master, Bhagavān's millions and millions of *śaktis* are waiting for His order. But it is not like our giving an order to someone. Bhagavān simply desires something in His mind and simultaneously that task is done. Here Kṛṣṇa thought, "Today Mother is trying to bind Me, but outside the cows are waiting for My *darśana*. Until I come, they will not give milk. The calves are also waiting for Me. The *sakhās* will come, and because I won't be able to go and play with them, they will be very unhappy."

The cowherd boys saw all of this and said, "Today Your mother has taught You a good lesson!" They were very unhappy that on that day they wouldn't be able to play with Kṛṣṇa, but at the same time they loved Kṛṣṇa so much that just by seeing Him very briefly they felt great happiness. Kṛṣṇa is very small in this pastime, only three-and-a-half years old. So these other boys are only three or even two years old, yet seeing Kṛṣṇa in this condition they felt great happiness. But they also lamented, "Oh, today Kṛṣṇa will not be able to play with us because Mother has bound Him."

This is *mugdhatā*, not *sarvajñatā*. This *svarūpa-śakti* is also called Yogamāyā, the energy by which Kṛṣṇa performs so many activities and pastimes. Yogamāyā saw that an opportunity for service was available, and she responded accordingly. "His waist will not be bound, and then He will be able to go and play." Regardless of how much rope was applied, the rope remained two fingers' length short. This is impossible, but it becomes possible by the arrangement of this *svarūpa-śakti*, the medium by which Bhagavān performs His pastimes.

What determines whether Yogamāyā gives the *darśana* of Bhagavān to someone or not? If Yogamāyā is pleased, then someone can receive Kṛṣṇa's *darśana*. If she is not pleased, then they won't get His *darśana*. This Yogamāyā is the foundation for all of His pastimes, and this same Yogamāyā in full form, expanded to the highest limit, is Śrīmatī Rādhikā Herself. The same *śakti* is present in Dvārakā in the forms of Satyabhāmā, Rukmiṇī and others, in Vaikuṇṭha in the forms of Lakṣmī, and in the heavenly planets in the forms of the wives of the plenary portions of Bhagavān there. In heaven there is the form of *cañcalā*, or restless, Lakṣmī, and in Vaikuṇṭha there is the form of *acañcalā*, or steady, Lakṣmī. They are all Śrīmatī Rādhikā's reflected forms or expansions.

In the material world there is *cañcalā* Lakṣmī. Why is she called that? Because today wealth is with one person, and tomorrow it will be with another. She doesn't stick to one husband, and she is always wandering in the four directions. Today here, tomorrow there, and so on. Who is she? She is the shadow *śakti* of the steady Lakṣmī: Bhū, Śrī and Nīlā. Durgā is also a shadow *śakti* – Vindyavāsinī, Kaṅkālī, Cāmuṇḍā and so on – they are all shadow *śaktis* of the steady Lakṣmī. At the time of Rāmacandra's pastimes, within Laṅkā there was Laṅkinī, and she was also a shadow *śakti* of the steady Lakṣmī. The demons were worshipping her, but by nature she was restless. When Hanumān came and attacked, she became perturbed and ran away, thinking, "Very soon he will destroy Rāvaṇa. This monkey has certainly come to defeat us."

In this world Lakṣmī is very restless, never remaining in one place. Some people who have abundant wealth think that they will turn it all over to their offspring, but there is no guarantee that it will stay within their family. But that Lakṣmī who in the form of Bhakti-devī resides with Bhagavān is steady. Wherever this Lakṣmī is, she is steady. If she is residing in a place where someone offends her, then she may leave; otherwise she will stay. But *bhakti* doesn't come quickly – it is very difficult to obtain. Therefore such superior potency (*para-śakti*) of Bhagavān cannot be understood by argument, but by the mood of service. If inside us is *niṣṭhā*, exclusive feelings towards one particular form of Bhagavān, then *bhakti* will come, but if there is not exclusive *niṣṭhā* towards one form, then it will not come.

One may desire to perform *bhajana* for Rāma and Sītā, Rādhā and Kṛṣṇa, Candrāvalī and Kṛṣṇa, and others. From the perspective of *tattva* this is all right, and it is possible that one may even attain

Vaikuṇṭha. But if there is not *niṣṭhā* for one particular deity, then there will be no *rasa* and no *ānanda*. This is being exclusive, but it is not being biased; it is thoroughly correct.

In the verse under discussion from *Bṛhad-bhāgavatāmṛta*, we find the word *parameśvarī*. Parameśvarī is *acintya-śakti*, and to know Her is not possible by argument. She is beyond that. When will we be able to have Her *darśana*? When we engage in exclusive *bhajana* it will become easy. The sentiment of the *gopīs*' *rāga-bhakti* is very rare, and very difficult to obtain. But although that sentiment is very rare, it can be achieved. Sometimes even if that thing which is considered the most degraded of all in this world is dovetailed in the service of Bhagavān, it can become the highest thing:

vikrīḍitaṁ vraja-vadhūbhir idaṁ ca viṣṇoḥ
śraddhānvito 'nuśṛṇuyād atha varṇayed yaḥ
bhaktiṁ parāṁ bhagavati pratilabhya kāmaṁ
hṛd-rogam āśv apahinoty acireṇa dhīraḥ

Śrīmad-Bhāgavatam (10.33.39)

Anyone who faithfully hears or describes the divine pastimes enjoyed by Śrī Kṛṣṇa with the *gopīs* of Vṛndāvana will very quickly obtain pure *bhakti*, thereby conquering the heart disease of lust.

There is a very beautiful explanation of this verse in the *Śrīmad-Bhāgavatam* commentary of Viśvanātha Cakravartī Ṭhākura. Some people think that they will first become free from all offences and *anarthas*, become pure by their own efforts, and then engage in *bhajana*, but that is absurd. First concentrate the mind and make the heart pure, then do *bhajana*, and then *bhakti* will come? It will never be like this. You can try to concentrate the mind for millions of lives, but there is no guarantee that it will remain focused. Even the senses of great sages like Viśvāmitra and Saubhari became disturbed, so therefore in millions of lives it will not be possible to control the mind by one's own personal endeavour. You will just be kept waiting for millions of lives. It is like thinking that you will wait until the water of a river dries up before you cross it. Whatever condition you are now in – if you are a thief, a dacoit, a hooligan or if you are pure – start performing *kṛṣṇa-bhajana* and chanting the holy name, and automatically *bhakti* will take care of the rest.

In this world, there is no greater misconduct than adultery, but if it is in relation to Kṛṣṇa, then it is not misconduct. Why? Because He is the husband of all. From the perspective of *bhakti* the feelings that the *gopīs* have for Kṛṣṇa are the highest of all sentiments, both in this world and in the spiritual world. Some people who hear the Tenth Canto of *Śrīmad-Bhāgavatam* say, "Hey, this is mundane! They are loving Kṛṣṇa through hiding and deception, and because of this they have become so exalted?"

Yes, they have become so exalted that the most exemplary personalities such as Nārada, Uddhava and the Kumāras meditate on the *gopīs*' feet within their hearts. Those devotees who have developed sentiments like those of the *gopīs* – *vikrīḍitam vraja-vadhūbhiḥ* – will gain entrance into Kṛṣṇa's playful pastimes.

If one listens with faith to narrations of Kṛṣṇa's pastimes with the *gopīs* by *anuśṛṇuyāt* – accepting a pure spiritual master, an ideal *rasika* Vaiṣṇava who knows the science of Kṛṣṇa, and then constantly hearing from him – then exclusive sentiment will come to him. This sentiment is our everything, and it will arise in us and give us great happiness. *Anuvarṇayet* means it is passed on from one to another. What Vyāsadeva taught to Śukadeva Gosvāmī, Śukadeva in turn taught that very same thing to Mahārāja Parīkṣit. And what Śukadeva Gosvāmī taught, Sūta Gosvāmī described that very same thing in the assembly of the sages. If it is described like this and one listens with faith, what will happen? *Bhaktiṁ parāṁ bhagavati: parām* means Kṛṣṇa, the best of all *tattva* – one will obtain *bhakti* for Him, and that *bhakti* will become so intense that *pratilabhya kāmaṁ hṛd-rogam āśu*: one will obtain the *prema* of the *gopīs*. And by obtaining that, what will happen? The disease in the heart will be uprooted. What is that disease? The lust that men and women have for one another, which clouds a person's intelligence. If it creates so much strife amongst lower species such as animals and birds, then what to speak of the effect it has on people?

This lust is so all-encompassing that when the desire comes for anything, we think, "I am its enjoyer. I am its master." Even in regard to such basic things as food and clothing – any desire for personal enjoyment whatsoever – it is all lust. There are so many types of lust from gross to subtle, but by hearing about the *gopīs*' transcendental desire for Kṛṣṇa, automatically the heart disease of worldly desire, which binds us birth after birth, can be uprooted. And then *prema*, that entity which couldn't be obtained by millions of lifetimes of attempts at purification by our own efforts, will gradually come. Just see how something that is degraded in the worldly sense can at once be made pure when performed for Bhagavān's pleasure.

Therefore, Viśvanātha Cakravartī Ṭhākura says, "To eradicate your bad qualities, to control your mind and to rid yourself of lust, all of your personal efforts will prove futile! In millions and millions of lives it will not happen! Just do one thing, and don't worry: practise devotion unto the Supreme Lord by engaging in hearing (*śravaṇam*), chanting (*kīrtanam*) and remembrance (*smaraṇam*). There are so many kinds of narrations about Kṛṣṇa, but the descriptions of the *rāsa-līlā* wherein Kṛṣṇa is sporting with the *gopīs* are the topmost. If someone becomes absorbed in them day and night, then he will find no free time for anything else. So how could he possibly become engaged in any sinful activity? That person is really *dhīraḥ* – one whose *buddhi*, intelligence, is fixed."

teṣāṁ satata-yuktānāṁ
bhajatāṁ prīti-pūrvakam
dadāmi buddhi-yogaṁ taṁ
yena mām upayānti te

Bhagavad-gītā (10.10)

To those who are sincerely devoted to serving Me with love, I give the understanding by which they can come to Me.

In this verse, the word *buddhi* means the intelligence that gives Bhagavān. It is full of mercy. In one place, Viśvanātha Cakravartī Ṭhākura says, "O Kṛṣṇa, You are very merciful. You said *dadāmi buddhi-yogam*. Please give me *buddhi-yoga*. And You may ask, 'Which *buddhi-yoga* do you want? The *buddhi-yoga* that I gave to Arjuna?' But I don't desire that. For Arjuna it was all right. For those people who desire that variety of *buddhi-yoga*, it is all right. But to me please give that *buddhi-yoga* by which even You become bewildered and forget Yourself, in which You sport with the *gopīs*, and by serving which one completely forgets himself. To become the servant of the *gopīs*, to become lost in that service and forget everything else – I want that *buddhi*. For those who are serving You, having forgotten everything else and being intoxicated in that service, You are doing everything in the form of an ordinary human being. Be merciful and please inspire that *buddhi-yoga* within me. Such *dhīraḥ*, steadiness, is what I desire. Give me that intelligence by which I can come to You in this way." Viśvanātha Cakravartī Ṭhākura has offered such a beautiful prayer to Bhagavān, and no one can offer a higher prayer than this.

Here Viśvanātha Cakravartī Ṭhākura is saying, "My friends, practise *sādhana* like this. Don't pray in this way all of the time: 'O Kṛṣṇa, I am a big thief, a big hooligan… .' Just become deeply absorbed in His pastimes. 'I am qualified, I am not qualified' – this is the consideration of a neutral person."

Let us say someone has become greedy for a *rasagullā*, and he has no money. Then by grabbing it, stealing it, or by any means he will get it. Our greed for *bhakti* must be like that, and we should pray to Bhagavān that He will be merciful and give us this greed. So the purport here is that the *buddhi-yoga* we really want is the mercy of Yogamāyā.

This Yogamāyā *śakti* of Bhagavān is *durvitarkyā* – inconceivable and beyond argument or debate. "Others have received it, so I should certainly receive it. Why was it given to them anyway? Bilvamaṅgala's conduct was very bad, so why did he get it? And on the contrary my consciousness is pure; I have never stolen or told a lie. Why shouldn't I get *bhakti*?" We should not think like this. "When will we get it? How will we get it?" – it is *durvitarkyā*, inconceivable.

By the arrangement of this very Yogamāyā alone, Bhagavān appears in unlimited varieties of forms. When Bhagavān comes in the forms of Nara and Nārāyaṇa, He is always absorbed in meditation. That is one *bhāva*, or mood. In the form of Rāma He has a particular mood, in all other forms He possesses a specific mood, and all of this is arranged by the influence of Yogamāyā, Parameśvarī. From Parameśvara comes Parameśvarī. The verse under discussion here from *Bṛhad-bhāgavatāmṛta* says *kintv asyaikānta-bhakteṣu, gūḍhaṁ kiñcin na tiṣṭhati*: even though it is inconceivable, still, it is not a secret to His pure devotees. By whose mercy will we obtain exclusive *bhakti*? From Yogamāyā we will receive a proper understanding of it; otherwise no one will ever be able to understand it.

Nārada told Gopa-kumāra, "To enter Goloka you must understand these points. Then you will be qualified to render service there. Otherwise you will remain here in Vaikuṇṭha and have dealings with Nārāyaṇa in a similar way as the Kumāras, who came here, received a brief *darśana*, and then merely returned to their own residence."

Now I will explain the next verse:

patnī-sahasrair yugapat praṇītaṁ
dravyaṁ sa bhuṅkte bhagavān yadaikaḥ
paśyanti tāny atra yathā pratisvam
ādau mamādatta tad eva me 'tti

Bṛhad-bhāgavatāmṛta (2.4.166)

Bhagavān Śrī Kṛṣṇa simultaneously ate all of the meals offered by His queens in such a way that each queen thought, "He has accepted His meal from me first."

Here Nārada is saying that once he went to Dvārakā and saw a very peculiar pastime of Kṛṣṇa. So many queens were there, including principal queens such as Rukmiṇī; Kṛṣṇa had thousands of wives there. They all prepared many different kinds of preparations, and they wanted to see whose offering Kṛṣṇa would consider the most beautiful and the most delicious. They all invited Kṛṣṇa to their respective palaces, and they were all watching to see whose palace He would go to first. They had already given invitations to Kṛṣṇa. It was understood that whomever could take Kṛṣṇa into their home on this day and serve Him drinks and feed Him would possess the topmost good fortune. Seeing Kṛṣṇa emerge with Nārada from the Sudharmā assembly hall, all the queens eagerly stepped out of their palaces. Nārada was thinking, "Whose palace will He go to first?"

Just then Kṛṣṇa assumed as many forms as there were queens and entered the palace of each and every one of them simultaneously. Nārada also expanded into as many forms and followed behind Him. This is also possible for great devotees; we shouldn't think them incapable of doing that. There is only one Rādhikā, but when Kṛṣṇa becomes Nārāyaṇa, She becomes Lakṣmī. When He becomes Vāmana, She becomes the Lakṣmī of Vāmana. And when He becomes Mahāprabhu, She expands into Viṣṇupriya and Lakṣmīpriya. In this way, wherever there will be pastimes, She will be there. When Sadāśiva becomes Śaṅkara, then She becomes Pārvatī.

It is the same for devotees who are *rasika*. Some devotees are satisfied in only one *līlā*, while others go to all *līlās* and, assuming many different forms, taste many different pastimes. Merely tasting one *līlā* will not satisfy them. Nārada is like this. For those who are *rasika*, it is difficult to say where they are. Nārada visits Nārāyaṇa, and in the same form he also goes to visit Rāma. But the Nārada that goes to Rāma is different from the Nārada that goes to visit Kṛṣṇa. Not different in *tattva*, but different in *bhāva*. Each of these expansions of Nārada has his own *sthāyibhāva*, permanent sentiment. Just as Kṛṣṇa says that He will never leave Vṛndāvana, it is like this with devotees also. The *gopīs* will never leave Vṛndāvana. If they do, it will only be in another form as expansions, and it is the same with the *gopas* also.

When Nārada enters Vraja-dhāma, he is Madhumaṅgala. At Govardhana at Nārada-kuṇḍa, near Kusuma-sarovara, he performs austerities and worship for what purpose? His desires have not been completely fulfilled. "O Kṛṣṇa, I have seen what it is to be in *sakhya-rasa*, I have seen what is in *vātsalya*, and I have also taken a look at *dāsya*. Now, O Lord, what is remaining?" He desires to experience that also, and taking another form, it may be possible.

So Nārada is saying that Kṛṣṇa came out of the Sudharmā assembly hall in this way, and that he was following Him. So many queens offered preparations, and Kṛṣṇa expanded into thousands of forms and simultaneously went to the palace of each and every queen. With the very same form and mood, He simultaneously tasted all their offerings. Some people say that there was only one form of Kṛṣṇa going from palace to palace very, very fast, but Nārada could not have done this as well. They say that with such great speed Kṛṣṇa went to each queen in such a way that all of the queens thought that He had come to her first. They say that if one minute is divided into millions of parts, that is the speed at which He was going. But it is like this only in His *mādhurya-līlā* in Vraja. In His *aiśvarya-līlā* in Dvārakā He expands into many forms, but in Vraja He doesn't expand into more forms; He remains in one form only. When Nārada saw Kṛṣṇa expand into all of these forms in His *aiśvarya-līlā*, he was not at all astonished. When was he really astonished? When he saw Kṛṣṇa in His *mādhurya-līlā*. With great speed and dexterity the same one Kṛṣṇa was appearing simultaneously between millions of *gopīs*, and each and every *gopī* was thinking, "Oh, Kṛṣṇa is very attracted to me! He loves me the most!"

Next Nārada speaks this verse (*Bṛhad-bhāgavatāmṛta* 2.4.167):

kvacit keṣv api jīveṣu
tat-tac-chakti-praveśataḥ
tasyāveśāvatārā ye
te 'pi tadvan matā budhaiḥ

When Bhagavān's potency enters into a living entity, he is known by the wise to be a *śaktyāveśa-avatāra*, an empowered incarnation.

If any special potency of Bhagavān enters into a living entity, he is called a *śaktyāveśa-avatāra*. This is the meaning of *śaktyāveśa-avatāra*: Bhagavān has transmitted His own transcendental potency (*bhagavattā-śakti*) into that person. Bhagavān is the possessor of all *śakti*, but *bhagavattā* is the manifestation of *śakti*. Bhagavān has unlimited qualities and this *śakti* manifests them all. Bhagavān is heroic, merciful, knowledgable and full in all six opulences, and they all manifest by *śakti*. Who really lifted Girirāja-Govardhana? *Śakti*, without whom His each and every activity would not take place. But we should not think that *śakti*, potency, and *śaktimān*, the possessor of the potency, are separate. They are one and the same.

We must respect those in whom *śakti* has entered just as we would respect incarnations of Bhagavān Himself. Paraśurāma, Nārada, Kapiladeva – we should give respect to them as empowered incarnations of Bhagavān because there *śakti* has manifested. Who is the *guru*? There are different gradations, but he is either Bhagavān's *jñāna-avatāra, bhakti-avatāra* or *prema-avatāra*:

sākṣād-dharitvena samasta-śāstrair
uktas tathā bhāvyata eva sadbhiḥ
kintu prabhor yaḥ priya eva tasya
vande guroḥ śrī-caraṇāravindam

Śrī Gurvaṣṭaka (7)

> The spiritual master is to be honoured as much as Bhagavān Himself because he is the most confidential servant of the Lord. This is acknowledged in all revealed scriptures and followed by all authorities. I offer obeisances to the lotus feet of such a *guru*.

If a Vaiṣṇava gives us *bhakti*, then what will we call him? What sentiment will we have towards him? He is giving us *śikṣā*, instruction, and although he may not have spoken the *mantra* in our ear, he is giving us *bhakti*. He is giving us something which is indescribable. Yadunandana Ācārya originally gave initiation to Raghunātha dāsa Gosvāmī, but is what Rūpa Gosvāmī gave him later to be considered less important than that? We should always consider these things. The *śakti* of Bhagavān is within the spiritual master, so we should respect him just as we respect Bhagavān. In reality even more credit should be given to the *guru*, because by his mercy we can understand Bhagavān. We have no direct knowledge of Bhagavān. Mahāprabhu was very merciful, but we can't say that we actually know Him. Bhaktivinoda Ṭhākura, Viśvanātha Cakravartī Ṭhākura, Rūpa Gosvāmī – we have heard that they were all very merciful, and they can give us mercy from their position, but it is our own *guru* who can give us special things because of our direct relationship with him. He attracts us to *bhakti* and eradicates our desires for material enjoyment, so therefore birth after birth we will remain indebted to him.

Chapter Eight

The Glories of Yogamāyā

Nārada Ṛṣi has explained to Gopa-kumāra that just as Bhagavān, being one, assumes different incarnations, His internal potency is also one but comes in different forms. According to her different activities, she is known by different names. In different forms this same potency is present in Dvārakā-purī, in Vaikuṇṭha with the various incarnations of Nārāyaṇa, and with the demigods.

It is written in some places that devotees don't desire the mercy of the Lakṣmī who is the goddess of *aiśvarya*, opulence. We should understand that this does not refer to the Mahā-Lakṣmī of Nārāyaṇa in the spiritual world. That Lakṣmī is not *cañcalā*, restless, but she is steady and permanent, and in that form she is perpetually serving Nārāyaṇa.

Cañcalā Lakṣmī was born from the churning of the milk ocean. This Lakṣmī is the goddess who embodies all money and wealth, and devotees don't desire her mercy. Even if she wants to serve devotees and fulfil their desires, they simply offer obeisances to her and leave. What to speak of older devotees, even new devotees are more dear than her to Bhagavān. Kṛṣṇa said:

na tathā me priyatama
ātma-yonir na śaṅkaraḥ
na ca saṅkarṣaṇo na śrīr
naivātmā ca yathā bhavān

Śrīmad-Bhāgavatam (11.14.15)

My dear Uddhava, neither Brahmā, Śaṅkara, Saṅkarṣaṇa, the goddess of fortune Lakṣmī, nor even My own self are as dear to Me as you are.

He has spoken this verse in relation to *cañcalā* Lakṣmī. If the Lakṣmī who is near Nārāyaṇa serving Him in Vaikuṇṭha were to hear this verse, what would she do? Therefore don't take this verse to be in relation to her. This can be said for the Lakṣmī who appeared as the daughter of Bhṛgu. Only a Vaiṣṇava who has attentively heard from the *guru-paramparā* will understand statements like these from the scriptures. Others will certainly misunderstand. Some may say that in this verse Lakṣmī is another name of Rādhikā, but that would mean that another devotee would be greater than Rādhikā – Uddhava would be a greater devotee than Her. Uddhava desires to take the dust of the *gopīs*' feet on his head, so to think that anyone is greater than Rādhikā, the very origin of all goddesses of fortune, would certainly be erroneous. In order to understand which Lakṣmī has been referred to in this verse requires some careful consideration. We must try to properly understand our *siddhānta*, and that can only be done by remaining in the association of Vaiṣṇavas.

This verse refers to the Lakṣmī that bestows mystic perfections, who gave opulence to Brahmā and the demigods, and who appeared from the churning of the ocean. What to speak of older devotees, even new devotees are superior to her. Devotees, liberated souls and those who desire liberation: these three types of people don't worship that goddess of wealth, *cañcalā* Lakṣmī. This verse is not referring to the Lakṣmī who is constantly situated at Bhagavān's chest, massaging His feet and serving Him. That Mahā-Lakṣmī is steady, not restless, and is very dear to Bhagavān. No devotee will ever be indifferent towards her. But if anyone aspires for the affectionate sidelong glance from the source of all incarnations, Śrī Kṛṣṇa, and His dearest Śrīmatī Rādhikā, then they will simply respect this Mahā-Lakṣmī but not beg for her mercy. They will beg for mercy directly from Śrīmatī Rādhikā Herself.

This is not to be considered disrespect; there is no place for disrespecting any Vaiṣṇavas. A Vaiṣṇava who is *rasika* and *tattvajña*, conversant with the science of Kṛṣṇa, should always be respected. But that doesn't mean that the remainder of Vaiṣṇavas should be disrespected. That will be an offence, *aparādha*. But we should be especially careful to commit no offence at the feet of Kṛṣṇa's exclusive *rasika, tattvajña* Vaiṣṇava, and with our hearts we will always aspire to serve him.

Suppose there is a festival going on and hundreds of devotees are there, including *uttama-adhikārī* Vaiṣṇavas, *madhyama-adhikārī* Vaiṣṇavas and *kaniṣṭha-adhikārī* Vaiṣṇavas. If amongst them there is an exclusive *rāgānuga* or even *rūpānuga* Vaiṣṇava, then we shall give more respect to him, but we will have to give it with cleverness. Otherwise ordinary people will think that they can be indifferent to *kaniṣṭha-adhikārī* and *madhyama-adhikārī* devotees. On three levels we shall accordingly offer respect, but with some cleverness. Appropriate respect must be shown to all, in gradation, just as Rūpa Gosvāmī has written:

kṛṣṇeti yasya giri taṁ manasādriyeta
dīkṣāsti cet praṇatibhiś ca bhajantam īśam
śuśrūṣayā bhajana-vijñam ananyam anya-
nindādi-śūnya-hṛdam īpsita-saṅga-labdhyā

Upadeśāmṛta (5)

The *uttama* Vaiṣṇava should be served with love. Being an exclusive devotee, he never criticises anyone. Whether he obtains happiness or unhappiness, he remains satisfied. He serves Kṛṣṇa exclusively by the topmost, radiant devotional mellow (*ujjvala-rasa*), so towards him we will have a special sentiment, but we will not disrespect anyone. One devotee we will criticise, another we will disobey, another we will disrespect – saving ourselves from this mentality we should give appropriate respect to all, and serve the advanced *rasika* Vaiṣṇava with love.

Yogamāyā has so many forms, and we should never commit any offence to any of them. We should give them appropriate respect because they are the *śakti* of Bhagavān, but we should not perform any give-and-take transactions with them. This should be the only taking: "Please give your mercy to us so our enjoying spirit will go away." Otherwise, this bartering mentality will lead us into material enjoyment. That should be our only prayer to them, and towards our most worshipful goddesses, the *gopīs*, we should have a mood of following and serving them.

In some places this potency of Bhagavān is known as *mahā-vibhūti*, in some places as Yogamāyā, and in some places as *ātma-māyā*. In *Bhagavad-gītā* (4.6) we find the words *sambhavāmy ātma-māyayā*: "I incarnate by My internal energy." What is the meaning of *ātma-māyā*? That potency of Bhagavān in His natural form. Where does this *ātma-māyā* come from? Who is its root? Śrīmatī Rādhikā. By the medium of this potency, *sac-cid-ānanda*, Bhagavān's enjoyment takes place. This Yogamāyā potency is eternal (*nitya*), factual (*satya*), beginningless (*anādi*) and unlimited (*ananta*). She took birth along with Kṛṣṇa, so how can she be *anādi*, beginningless? Prior to her own birth, she arranged for Baladeva Prabhu to appear as the seventh child in the womb of Devakī and then she herself took birth from the womb of Yaśodā later. So because she performed some activity before taking birth, she is eternal, and is therefore known as Sanātanī.

This Yogamāyā is the one who increases *bhajanānanda*, the happiness experienced by Kṛṣṇa's servants. This Yogamāyā, taking the essence of the *hlādinī* and *saṁvit* potencies together, takes a devotee progressively through the stages of *śraddhā*, *bhāva*, *prema* and all the way up to *mahābhāva*. As if feeding the devotees milk, she nurtures them in so many ways, and she arranges for a soul who has attained perfection in *sādhana* to appear in the womb of a *gopī*. The personification of that Yogamāyā, Paurṇamāsī, is the mother of Sāndīpani Muni and resides in Nandagrāma. In many ways she increases *rasa*, either by providing a stimulus, or by personally doing so as Paurṇamāsī. She increases Yaśodā's *vātsalya-rasa*, she increases the cowherd boys' *sakhya-rasa*, and she increases the *dāsya-bhāva* of those in that *rasa*. She enhances all of the *rasas* and nurtures all living entities. She is the mother of variegated *bhajanānanda*, and if one doesn't take shelter of her, his *bhakti* cannot increase.

This Yogamāyā is the foundation of the Lord's many kinds of incarnations. She makes all the arrangements in regard to Bhagavān's dress, appearance, ornaments and pastimes. On one of the many occasions when Kṛṣṇa played the flute, the *gopīs* went into a state of bewilderment. Some were wearing ornaments in the wrong places, and others placed make-up in places where it should not have been applied. They were in varying awkward conditions. Who arranged all of this? Yogamāyā. Their state of disarray increased their beauty one million times. Yogamāyā was the cause of this. Suppose one *gopī* puts an ankle bracelet around her neck, and a necklace around her ankle. When she goes before Kṛṣṇa, He will see it and say, "Oh, you have arranged your ornaments so beautifully!" So tell me then: how much more valuable has it become? The cause is Yogamāyā.

This potency of the Lord is *durvitarkyā*: inconceivable. Through Yogamāyā, Kṛṣṇa performs pastimes with His devotees, there is His *mugdhatā* (being spellbound in emotion), the *mugdhatā* of Yaśodā and all varieties of pastimes. From the very beginning it is done by her for the pleasure of Bhagavān and His devotees. In another form called Mahāmāyā, the activities of the demons are facilitated and the *jīvas* are bound within material existence.

Vasudeva took Kṛṣṇa to Gokula and brought the girl Yogamāyā back from the bed of Yaśodā. As long as she was with Vasudeva, she remained as Yogamāyā; but when she arrived in the jail of

Kaṁsa, and Kaṁsa lifted her up to kill her, then the activities of Mahāmāyā began, and Yogamāyā, in an invisible form, began her own activities. Exactly when she changed to her shadow form, no one knew. Seeing this, it must appear to most persons that they are one and the same potency, but they are not one. When she was placed in the jail and Kaṁsa grabbed her, she became eight-armed Durgā. He became astonished and frightened, and said, "Oh, you are directly my worshipful goddess!" But ultimately, at what point she left her form as Yogamāyā, and how she did this and that – it is all *durvitarkyā*, inconceivable.

The potency of Bhagavān is eternal, factual, beginningless, unlimited and indescribable. It cannot be fully described in words and an ordinary man cannot portray its form. Only an elevated, liberated, great soul can describe a little of it. Otherwise it cannot be described at all.

We know that we are not the body. Hundreds of thousands of times we have spoken this fact to others, but then we perform some sensual activity and again we forget this. If for one second we forget that we are not this body, then all of our determination for spiritual advancement may vanish. It happened to such a great liberated personality as Nārada. In the *Rāmāyaṇa* it is said that he was the cause of the appearance of Rāmacandra.[3] Selfishness for one penny can drown us in mundane consciousness. We must remain strong in *bhajana*, and with great humility we should perform *sādhana-*

---

3 Once Nārada desired to marry a princess, and in order to be successful at her *svayaṁvara*, he prayed to Viṣṇu for a face as beautiful as His. But to protect the *bhakti* of His devotee, Viṣṇu instead gave Nārada the face of a monkey. Not understanding why everyone was ridiculing him at the *svayaṁvara*, Nārada was then told to go and look at his reflection in a pond. Realising that Viṣṇu had deceived him, he cursed Viṣṇu that in His next life He would lose His wife, and that He would have to take the help of monkeys to get her back. Therefore Nārada is said to be the cause of the descent of Śrī Rāmacandra.

bhajana. Only by the influence of this Yogamāyā – when this potency is transmitted into the heart of a living entity – will the sentiment of *bhakti* arise, and we will be able to properly engage in the limbs of devotion headed by hearing and chanting. How is it done? By the essence of the *hlādinī* and *saṁvit* potencies together this sentiment arises in the heart of a *jīva*. This is called *viśuddha-sattva*, and this is the activity of Yogamāyā. She performs unlimited types of service in Vaikuṇṭha, Dvārakā, Mathurā and finally in Vṛndāvana.

There are differences in *bhakti*, and also differences in *rasa*. What are the differences in *bhakti*? *Sādhana-bhakti, bhāva-bhakti, vaidhī-bhakti, rāgānuga-bhakti*, and within them also are *niṣṭhā, ruci, āsakti, bhāva*, and next, in *nitya-siddha* devotees or in *sādhana-siddha* devotees are *sneha, māna, praṇaya, rāga, anurāga, bhāva* and *mahābhāva*. This variegatedness is all arranged by Yogamāyā. *Bhakti* is one; *bhakti* is not two. It is one sentiment, even though externally we see that there are sixty-four kinds, or nine kinds, or five kinds, or three kinds. *Rasa* is also one. *Rasa* is not many, but according to the different fields of activity of *sādhakas*, it appears to be in different forms. *Śṛṅgāra* is one complete *rasa, mādhurya-rasa*. Manifest from that in sequence are *vātsalya, sakhya* and *dāsya*, and it appears in those forms. Bhagavān is one, not two, but according to the gradation of one's devotion and the gradation of one's knowledge, He appears as Brahman, Paramātmā, Bhagavān, Kṛṣṇa and so many other forms. The same moon, according to our angle of vision, appears as the lunar days of *dvitīyā, trayodaśī, pañcamī* and so on – the moon doesn't change. It is the same moon; only our vision of it changes. Therefore sometimes it is *amāvasyā*, the new moon night, sometimes it is *pūrṇimā*, the full moon, and in precisely the same way, the same Bhagavān appears differently according to the gradation in a devotee's *sādhana*. Similarly, Bhagavān's potency is also seen according to the gradation in a devotee's *sādhana*. All of this variegatedness is the arrangement of Yogamāyā, and therefore for Yogamāyā there are so many *mantras*:

śrī-paurṇamāsyaś caraṇāravindaṁ
vande sadā bhakti-vitāna-hetum
śrī-kṛṣṇa-līlābdhi-taraṅga-magnaṁ
yasya manaḥ sarva-niṣevitāyāḥ

I offer obeisances to the lotus feet of Śrī Paurṇamāsī-devī, who is Bhagavān's Yogamāyā potency. She expands pure *prema-bhakti* for the feet of Śrī Rādhā-Kṛṣṇa, and her mind is always immersed in the ocean of Kṛṣṇa's pastimes.

kātyāyani mahā-māye
mahā-yoginy adhīśvari
nanda-gopa-sutaṁ devi
patiṁ me kuru te namaḥ

Śrīmad-Bhāgavatam (10.22.4)

[The *gopīs* worshipped Yogamāyā with this *mantra*:] O goddess Kātyāyanī, you are the great internal potency of Bhagavān, the possessor of all mystic power and the ultimate controller. Please make the son of Nanda our husband. We offer obeisances to you.

All of the variegatedness in Bhagavān's pastimes is arranged by Yogamāyā. Although the influence of this potency is indescribable, it is known to pure devotees, and they can describe it. Just as the glories of Bhagavān are indescribable, the glories of this potency are also indescribable, but knowing something of it, Bhagavān's pure devotees have described it. Śukadeva Gosvāmī, Vyāsa, Parāśara, Nārada, Rūpa and Sanātana Gosvāmīs, Jīva Gosvāmī – many *ācāryas* have described it.

sā parāparayoḥ śaktyoḥ
parā śaktir nigadyate
prabhoḥ svābhāvikī sā hi
khyātā prakṛtir ity api

Bṛhad-bhāgavatāmṛta (2.4.178)

> Bhagavān's potencies are classified either as superior or inferior. Yogamāyā is His superior, internal potency, and because she is Bhagavān's natural potency, in some places she is known by the name Prakṛti.

This Yogamāyā and Mahāmāyā are called the *parā*, superior, and *aparā*, inferior, potencies, respectively. They are perceived as two forms. Actually they are one, but the original is *parā*, and its shadow is *aparā*. What is the meaning of "shadow"? That which is non-different from the original but does not perform the same functions, is called a shadow. But not like the shadow of a tree which performs no activity. Our shadow also performs no activity, but the shadow of Bhagavān's potency is not inactive. In Goloka, Kṛṣṇa's *rāsa-līlā*, Kṛṣṇa's taking birth, devotees serving Kṛṣṇa, Kṛṣṇa's form, the *gopīs'* forms, the trees and plants there – everything is manifest by the influence of Yogamāyā and is true and eternal. And what are the activities of the *apara-śakti*? In different places in nature, by the action of this potency, some things are unreal, and some things are temporary. Some things are *satya*, real, and some things are *asatya*, false. All the relationships that we create in this world are false, whereas all of the objects of this world are true, but temporary.

Shells from the ocean are real, and silver is also real, but the illusion of thinking the shells to be silver is *asatya*, unreal. These shells glitter just like silver, and both of these things are real. The seer is also real. Three things are real, but considering these shells to be silver is unreal. Or when there is a rope, a snake and a seer, these three things are also real, but the illusion of considering the rope to be a snake is unreal. At night, when we are walking along in the dark, we may step on a rope. Because it is a little stiff, it wraps around our foot and we cry out, "Snake! Snake!" Then with a lamp we take a look, and our fear disappears. We may have thought that a snake had bitten us and that we were going to die, but after some light comes, that illusion is dispelled.

All of us are undoubtedly real, but to take it that "I am this body" is illusion. And to think that "all of these objects belong to me" is also illusion. What is "mine"? "I belong to Kṛṣṇa, and I am His servant." Up to this point our conception is real. We should consider all objects as instruments to be employed in the service of Bhagavān, but instead we think, "I am their master." On account of this, so much quarrelling and fighting is going on. *Sādhus* generally consider that nothing belongs to them, but when necessity for a certain object arises, even they claim ownership over it and fight amongst themselves.

Therefore, this *māyā-śakti* is very peculiar. This potency is one, but the external potency binds the *jīva* in an illusory conception of himself and his surroundings, whereas the internal potency, Yogamāyā, illuminates within the *jīva* the knowledge of things related to Bhagavān and *bhakti*. We may pray to Mahāmāyā, "Please be merciful to us. Now we are a little entrapped in your illusion, but we pray to you for *bhakti* to the feet of Kṛṣṇa." This Mahāmāyā, Kāmākhyā-devī, honestly and affectionately gave Gopa-kumāra the *gopāla-mantra*. Although displaying the form of Mahāmāyā, she performed the function of Yogamāyā. This potency in the form of Yogamāyā acts to benefit devotees, but if someone honestly desires it, then even in the form of Mahāmāyā this potency will show mercy to devotees. Otherwise, Mahāmāyā cheats the conditioned soul. At first, which potency came to Haridāsa Ṭhākura in the form of a prostitute? Mahāmāyā. Next, after she became a devotee, her activities were those of Yogamāyā. In all of these things we should see the difference and non-difference according to the *siddhānta* given by Caitanya Mahāprabhu, *acintya-bhedābheda*.

The living entity has also been called *para-śakti*. *Bhagavad-gītā* (7.5) says:

apareyam itas tv anyāṁ
prakṛtiṁ viddhi me parām
jīva-bhūtāṁ mahā-bāho
yayedaṁ dhāryate jagat

Besides these, O mighty-armed Arjuna, there is another, superior energy of Mine, which is the living entities who are exploiting the resources of the material, inferior nature.

How many *prakṛti*, or natures, does the Lord have? One. Bhagavān's natural potency – *svābhāvikī* – means *para-śakti*. But by saying *prakṛti*, we understand it to refer to the inferior nature, which creates this temporary world composed of eight elements. By saying *māyā* we are referring to *ātma-māyā*, the internal potency, but people in general don't know this, so the material world is usually known as *māyā*. The activities of the shadow potency Mahāmāyā are generally either false or temporary, whereas all the many activities of Yogamāyā are eternal.

Where does Mahāmāyā, the goddess who embodies this potency that makes the souls consider their bodies to be their actual selves, herself reside? Within the eighth material covering of the universe. Her complexion is very dark (*śyāma*); there, all is *śyāma*. In a very beautiful and attractive form she is situated there, and previously in that very place she met Gopa-kumāra. With some gifts to offer, she came before Gopa-kumāra and said, "Tell me what you desire. Do you desire *bhakti*? Then I will give you *bhakti*. Do you want facility to enjoy material happiness? Then I will give you all material happiness. I can give you everything, including *bhakti*, because I am the sister of Bhagavān. I will give you whatever you desire."

By her mercy, Gopa-kumāra emerged from there and again returned to the Earth planet. Otherwise it is not possible to come out from there. By our own effort it is not possible to overcome our illusion, and we just simply become more entrapped. Therefore we should depend fully on the grace of the Vaiṣṇavas, the spiritual master and Bhagavān, and we should not try on our own to escape this entrapment.

Next, Nārada told Gopa-kumāra, "Here in Vaikuṇṭha, you will see many different incarnations. One type is *vyaṣṭi*, and one is *samaṣṭi*." Who is the *samaṣṭi-avatāra*? Kṛṣṇa Himself. As we are *vyaṣṭi-jīvas*, and the *samaṣṭi-jīva* is Hiraṇyagarbha Brahmā, there are so many expanded incarnations such as Kūrma, Varāha, Nṛsiṁha, Paraśurāma and Vāmana, but don't consider Kṛṣṇa to be like Them. Kṛṣṇa is *samaṣṭi* – the seed, the root of all incarnations – and from this original seed, different forms come. From a mango seed, a *nīma* tree will not come, nor will bananas or guavas come from this mango seed. But Kṛṣṇa is such a seed that He is the seed of everything; such a very wonderful seed is Kṛṣṇa. Therefore He expands into all of the incarnations by His *acintya-śakti*. This is possible only for Kṛṣṇa and no one else. Nārāyaṇa may also have incarnations; for some purpose an incarnation may emerge from Him, but the special difference between Him and Kṛṣṇa is that even if Nārāyaṇa does assume an incarnation, He will not perform variegated pastimes. Kṛṣṇa is *avatārī*, the source of all incarnations, and when He personally descends, He performs unlimited variegated pastimes. Plus Kṛṣṇa possesses four extra special qualities of *mādhurya* that Nārāyaṇa does not.

Nārada is explaining all of this to Gopa-kumāra. "You desire to witness all of these pastimes, but how will you see them here?" Not aloud, but secretly Nārada is telling him. "Kṛṣṇa can do the work of the Vāmana incarnation. Alone, Kṛṣṇa can do the work of all the Viṣṇu incarnations, the *manvantara* incarnations, the *śaktyāveśa-avatāras*, the *līlā-avatāras* – anything that Nārāyaṇa does, Kṛṣṇa can do also. No one else can do all of this: it is a special quality of Kṛṣṇa."

The word *bhagavān* means what? *Bhaga* means 'opulences' – six in all – and *vān* means 'He who possesses them'. Many men of this world possess some opulence, but complete opulence is found only in Nārāyaṇa or in His incarnations. And where is opulence more complete? In Kṛṣṇa of Dvārakā and Mathurā. And where is opulence the most complete? In Vrajendra-nandana. There we find full wealth (*aiśvarya*), strength (*vīrya*), fame (*yaśa*), beauty (*śrī*), knowledge (*jñāna*) and renunciation (*vairāgya*).

aiśvaryasya samagrasya
vīryasya yaśasaḥ śriyah
jñāna-vairāgyayoś cāpi
ṣaṇṇāṁ bhaga itīṅganā

Viṣṇu Purāṇa (6.5.74)

All of these qualities are found in Nārāyaṇa and the incarnations also. Like *aiśvarya* – what is the opulence of Vāmanadeva? He appeared very small, but at the time of measuring the Earth, He immediately became wonderfully huge and in three steps covered the entire universe. This is *aiśvarya*. Rāmacandra, taking all of the monkeys and bears with Him, attacked Laṅkā and cut off Rāvaṇa's head, but a new head emerged. Each time He cut off Rāvaṇa's head, it would return. Finally He made a plan where by cutting off Rāvaṇa's ten heads, they would not return, and Rāvaṇa was killed. This is *aiśvarya*. Dvārakādhīśa Kṛṣṇa possesses so much opulence, and all of the other incarnations possess so much opulence, but Kṛṣṇa's opulence is especially marvellous. As a small boy He was at the breast of Pūtanā, drinking and drinking, and no one knew what He was actually doing. He wouldn't leave her breast, so they thought that maybe He was only playing. Then He sucked out her life. He was thinking, "I don't like anyone to come to Vṛndāvana and then leave again. She has entered within the boundaries of Vraja, therefore I will not allow her to ever leave."

This is *aiśvarya*, and it reaches its zenith in Kṛṣṇa. There is some renunciation (*vairāgya*) in Rāma: He left His kingdom, but He didn't leave Sītā – He left together with her. Kṛṣṇa's *vairāgya* is such that hundreds of thousands of *gopīs* were collected together at a very pure place, and a cool breeze was blowing; both *kiśora* and *kiśorīs* were there, but at once He disappeared. Kṛṣṇa had such a strong feeling of *vairāgya* that right before His eyes, fifty-six million members of the Yadu dynasty took canes and sticks and fought and killed one another – even His own son was finished and fell to the ground, yet Kṛṣṇa, neither smiling, nor worrying, nor saving anyone, just sat quietly with His legs crossed. Why? His vision was that all of this fighting and killing was just an *indrajāla*, a magical illusion. Therefore the pinnacle of all six opulences is found only in Kṛṣṇa. *Śrīmad-Bhāgavatam* (1.3.28) says:

ete cāṁśa-kalāḥ puṁsaḥ
kṛṣṇas tu bhagavān svayam

All of these incarnations are either plenary portions or parts of plenary portions of the *puruṣa-avatāras*, but Kṛṣṇa is Bhagavān Himself.

Nārada told Gopa-kumāra, "Svayam Bhagavān Kṛṣṇa's pastimes are variegated, His affection is variegated, His *prema* is variegated, and His associates are variegated. Anyone who has had even half of a taste of this immense variegatedness by hearing about it simply cannot remain here in Vaikuṇṭha."

Chapter Nine

Kṛṣṇa Gives Prema Even To His Enemies

Gopa-kumāra was somewhat dissatisfied with Vaikuṇṭha – that Vaikuṇṭha which is so desirable, where very, very beautiful *bhakti* is going on, and which is so difficult to attain. When Gopa-kumāra arrived there, Nārāyaṇa engaged him in the service of fanning Him with a *cāmara*. Sometimes He even displayed the form of Gopāla and the *līlā* of taking the cows out to graze and other pastimes also, but still Gopa-kumāra was not happy there.

I knew of one man who from childhood was hankering to go to Vṛndāvana from his residence in the state of Bihar. He was thinking, "When will I be able to go to Vṛndāvana? There I will bathe in the Yamunā, I will roll in the *kuñjas*; sometimes I will go to Rādhā-kuṇḍa, and sometimes I will go to Śyāma-kuṇḍa." After a very long time the opportunity finally arrived, and leaving everything behind, he went to Vṛndāvana and stayed for some time. At first, with great emotion he roamed in the four directions, smearing dust on himself and everything. Then after some time, something astonishing happened: gradually his 'fever' decreased. It is like a fever, isn't it? "I will go to Vṛndāvana, I will go to Govardhana, I will go to Rādhā-kuṇḍa." At first his fever had increased, and so he left everything and came to Vṛndāvana. He visited all the places of Kṛṣṇa's pastimes and daily he visited numerous temples and went on *parikramā*. Sometimes he would even do *parikramā* two or three times in the same day. He did whatever he was physically capable of doing, but then after some time the low tide of his fever came, and he didn't perform any *parikramā* or visit any temples.

Some come to Vṛndāvana and without understanding anything they say, "This is the fruit of one or two births' *sādhana*, in Vṛndāvana?" But others come and see that Vṛndāvana is full of *rasa*, and upon residing here for a short time, they become overwhelmed with *bhāva*. But for those who are newcomers and don't have such internal development, what will they see in the dust and stone of Vṛndāvana? Everything they come across will only disturb their minds, and this will be their *darśana* of Vṛndāvana.

But Gopa-kumāra's mind was disturbed in Vaikuṇṭha for a different reason. In his heart there was some ardent desire; intense spiritual greed produces this type of ardent desire. And how did it come? For millions of years he had been practising *sādhana*: he had been to Brahmaloka and many other worlds and back again, and millions of years had elapsed. His ardent desire didn't come after only one day; it came only after performing *bhajana* by way of the *gopāla-mantra*, like the method of Brahmā. In our *sampradāya* it is one of the main *mantras*, yet still he was not feeling completely fulfilled.

Vaikuṇṭha is the pinnacle attained by *vaidhī-bhakti* and is not minimised in our scriptures. Up to the Ninth Canto of *Śrīmad-Bhāgavatam* it is said to be the highest destination. Where was Ajāmila taken? What was the destination of Prahlāda? Vaikuṇṭha. And what was the destination of Dhruva? Dhruvaloka, meaning one extended part of Vaikuṇṭha. Therefore it has been stated that there is no higher place to be attained by performing *bhakti*. Although in one or two places in the scriptures we find the glories of Goloka Vraja described, they have been described so briefly that an ordinary person will not understand Goloka's true value; only one who can extract the essence will see, not everyone. Obtaining residence there is extremely rare, and within Gopa-kumāra's heart is that rare desire for *darśana* of Gopāla. Along with that he desires *kṛṣṇa-prema* that is unrestricted like a horse with no reins.

What is unrestricted *prema?* The members of Śrīmatī Rādhikā's family bound Her inside the house, and the other *gopīs* were also bound inside their homes. "If you go to meet Kṛṣṇa we will punish you! Serve your husband or we will beat you! And we will spread your bad name everywhere!" *Prema* with fear of worldly reaction due to having failed to uphold one's *dharma* is restricted love; but the *gopīs* left their husbands regardless to be with Kṛṣṇa. Their *prema* was not bound; rather it was fully manifested, and it even increased further. Many obstacles will come, yet *prema* will surely cross over them and heighten one's desire to meet Kṛṣṇa. Therefore so many people were given obstacles, their desire for meeting Kṛṣṇa increased, and they finally met Him. Where there is a mood of awe and reverence (*aiśvarya-bhāva*), there is no place for such *prema*. If Bhagavān manifests His nature as the Supreme, He will not freely converse with any ladies and He will not approach any young, unmarried girl. Would Rāmacandra even look upon the face of an unmarried girl? Would Śrī Caitanya Mahāprabhu after He accepted *sannyāsa*? What to speak of not noting what ornaments they would be wearing around their necks or on their wrists, Mahāprabhu would not even look at the nails of their toes! Although They are Bhagavān, still They possess such shyness and *dharmajña*, constant awareness of upholding Their *dharma*.

Where there is such a sentiment, *prema* is restricted, but this obstacle is due to the nature of one's own worshipful Lord. Obstacles imposed by others are not enough to be a problem. All such obstacles were placed before Gopa-kumāra. In Vaikuṇṭha, the residents teased him: "You keep saying 'Gopāla, Gopāla, Kṛṣṇa,' and you say that while holding a piece of bamboo stick Kṛṣṇa will engage in the *rāsa* dance with the *gopīs*? This is a very shameful thing. Will Nārāyaṇa ever do this?" But this is not the problem, the obstacle. Then why is Gopa-kumāra dissatisfied? Nārada told him the reason. "In the form of Nārāyaṇa, He will not manifest the type of *prema* that you desire; He simply will not give it. You will not be able to laugh with Him, converse freely with Him – that is the big obstacle to *prema* here."

Before, when Nārada Ṛṣi told Gopa-kumāra to remain in Vaikuṇṭha for some time, he wanted him to understand all of this *tattva*. Nārāyaṇa has a total of sixty qualities, five more than the demigods. Of these five, the first is His being *hatāri-gati-dāyaka*: He gives a high destination to those killed by His own hand. The second is that He possesses the highest pinnacle of all *aiśvarya*. The third is that He is the original seed of all different incarnations. The fourth is that He is the attractor of even the liberated souls, and the fifth is that He is eternally present in millions of universes. Therefore Nārāyaṇa is also Bhagavān and *avatārī*, the seed of all incarnations. Kṛṣṇa is also *avatārī*, so what is the difference between Them? When we say that Nārāyaṇa doesn't come as an *avatāra*, we mean that His selfsame form that is present in Vaikuṇṭha will not come to this world. Hayagrīva and other incarnations come, but Nārāyaṇa Himself – with club, lotus flower, disc and conchshell in His four hands – comes in another form as someone's son, husband, brother or friend, and then performs all His pastimes from those positions. And Kṛṣṇa? Bringing Vṛndāvana-dhāma with Him, He descends in His original form, playing the flute and enjoying with the *gopīs*. Bringing His *dhāma* and associates, He descends in His selfsame form.

The Nārāyaṇa present at Badarī-Nārāyaṇa in the form of Nara and Nārāyaṇa is different from *vaikuṇṭha-adhipati* Nārāyaṇa, the master of Vaikuṇṭha. When Nārāyaṇa came here as Vāmana, Lakṣmī also came here, but it was Vāmana Nārāyaṇa that came here, and in Vaikuṇṭha-dhāma there was still *vaikuṇṭha-adhipati* Nārāyaṇa. Kāraṇodakaśāyī Viṣṇu, lying on Śeṣa, is also Nārāyaṇa, but His form and activities are different. The form and activities of the original Nārāyaṇa of Vaikuṇṭha are not brought to this world. Therefore it is said that there is no actual incarnation of Nārāyaṇa Himself. But in His original form as a *kiśora*, Kṛṣṇa descends bringing His associates, His *līlā*, and the entire sixty-four-square-mile Vraja-maṇḍala, which includes Rādhā-kuṇḍa, Śyāma-kuṇḍa, Girirāja-Govardhana, Nandagrāma and Varṣāṇā. This is His special characteristic; Nārāyaṇa doesn't do this. This is Kṛṣṇa's unique characteristic as the *avatārī*.

Bhagavān has so many forms, and all are *hatāri-gati-dāyaka*. What does that mean? Those demons and enemies who are personally killed by Him are given a high destination. Rāmacandra, Nṛsiṁha, Varāha, Paraśurāma and all other incarnations are *hatāri-gati-dāyaka*. The five qualities that are found in Bhagavān and not found in the demigods are found to the highest degree in Kṛṣṇa. In Nārāyaṇa and the incarnations these qualities are complete (*pūrṇa*), but in Kṛṣṇa they are most complete (*pūrṇatama*). When any incarnation from Nārāyaṇa up to Nṛsiṁha kills someone, what destination do They give to those They have killed? Sutala, Svarga, Brahmaloka, all kinds of destinations. And They will also give liberation, *mukti*, to some enemies killed by Them. According to how someone has approached Them, They will give a particular destination to that person.

For example, in *rāma-līlā* there was Śarbaṅga Ṛṣi, who was worshipping the impersonal *brahma*. He heard that Rāmacandra was coming, and thinking that Rāma was the personification of *brahma*, he waited for Him. After the sage waited for some time, Rāmacandra finally came and gave His *darśana* to him. Being very pleased, the sage said, "O Lord, give me my desired destination." Then from the sage's body a light came out, and that light entered into the body of Rāmacandra and the sage attained liberation. He was such an unfortunate man: he received the direct *darśana* of Rāmacandra and he merely asked for liberation! Therefore Rāma will give liberation. Many incarnations will give it, but to those who approach Them as enemies, these incarnations will not give *prema*.

What is real liberation? According to *Śrīmad-Bhāgavatam* it is *svarūpeṇa vyavasthitiḥ*: that liberation which bestows service to the feet of Bhagavān, which is the highest destination. Those incarnations will not give this type of *mukti*. Especially They will not give it to those enemies whom They have killed. Nṛsiṁha killed Hiraṇyakaśipu, and Varāha killed Hiraṇyākṣa, yet neither of these demons obtained liberation in that birth. But Kṛṣṇa killed numerous demons and not only gave them liberation, to some He even gave *prema*! Like Pūtanā: she approached Kṛṣṇa in the guise of a mother, so He gave her a motherly position in Vraja. She didn't directly become Kṛṣṇa's mother; she was given a position in Goloka as an elderly *dāsī*, one who feeds Kṛṣṇa milk. Otherwise there would be a problem – she would be equal to Yaśodā, but that isn't the case. She went to Goloka as a *dāsī*. This type of liberation Kṛṣṇa can give, and no other incarnation can give it.

Those that are killed by Bhagavān are generally given ordinary destinations, but don't think that He doesn't give liberation as well. He can give liberation, and to devotees He gives *prema*. Citraketu Mahārāja didn't desire liberation, and so he prayed:

na nāka-pṛṣṭhaṁ na ca pārameṣṭhyaṁ
na sārva-bhaumaṁ na rasādhipatyam
na yoga-siddhīr apunar-bhavaṁ vā
samañjasa tvā virahayya kāṅkṣe

Śrīmad-Bhāgavatam (6.11.25)

O Bhagavān, I do not desire to attain Dhruvaloka or Brahmaloka, nor do I desire to rule over the middle or lower planetary systems.

> I also do not desire the mystic perfections of *yoga*, nor liberation from the cycle of repeated birth and death if it means being separated from You.

Nṛsiṁhadeva offered liberation to Prahlāda Mahārāja, but Prahlāda didn't desire it. In this way devotees don't desire liberation, but if anyone wants it, Bhagavān can give it. And He gives *prema* to those who worship Him with a desire for it, like the royal princesses of Janakapura. They wanted Rāma to marry them and become their husband, so He showed them the path: "I can only accept one wife; therefore all of you will take birth in *kṛṣṇa-līlā* in the wombs of *gopīs*, and there your desires will be fulfilled." Those great sages of Dandakaranya also first had to take birth as *gopīs* in Gokula; they were not sent directly to Goloka. Their identities as *gopīs* had not yet developed, so they had to first reside in the Vraja of this world for some time.

When a man takes a law course and passes the magistrate exams, will he then immediately become a judge? He will first have to undergo practical training by staying with an established judge for some time, and then he can become a judge himself. Similarly, going to the Vraja of this world, one will have to first undergo an apprenticeship, meaning that he must learn from someone, personally. For example, if a newly married girl goes to the house of her mother-in-law and hasn't yet learned how to cook, clean pots and serve food, then every day she will have to take abuse. But the members of the household will teach her everything. The mother-in-law will say, "My daughter, today my health is not so good. You do the cooking. Also, scrub the pots and sweep a little. I must rest, so you make some *roṭīs* like this...." Through such cleverness they will give her all practical instruction. In the same way, where will one receive this practical instruction to serve as a *gopī*? In the manifest pastimes of Bhagavān in Gokula Vraja, not at any other place. In a practical way, in the company of the eternally perfected devotees, for some time one will undergo an apprenticeship and learn. If one were sent directly to Goloka, then his identity would not yet be fully developed. Therefore it is necessary to first take birth in the manifest Vraja, and regardless of whether one will be in *dāsya*, *sakhya*, *vātsalya* or *mādhurya*, he must learn his duties there.

Next Nārada spoke this verse to Gopa-kumāra:

tāratamyaṁ tu kalpyeta
sva-sva-sevānusārataḥ
tat-tad-rasa-sajātīya-
sukha-vaicitryāpekṣayā

Bṛhad-bhāgavatāmṛta (2.4.193)

Kṛṣṇa has His uniqueness, and His associates, those who serve Him, also have their special characteristics. Kṛṣṇa is the crown jewel of those who are *āptakāma* and *ātmārāma*. He is like a white conchshell. If you place a pink flower in a white conchshell, its unique features will stand out, as would the qualities of any coloured flower placed in a white conchshell. The shelter of Kṛṣṇa is then in relation to the particular nature of the eternal associate. According to their uniqueness in *rasa*, Kṛṣṇa manifests in that same way and accepts their service.

For example, Varāha Bhagavān's service is being performed in Vaikuṇṭha, and there His desire is being fulfilled. Varāhadeva also has another form within *prakṛti*, in the eighth material covering. There He has assumed a very beautiful form, and millions and millions of souls are serving Him. And does Rāmacandra have only one or two eternal associates? He has millions. A very few of them are in *sakhya-rasa*, but mostly they serve Him in *dāsya-rasa*. And Vāmanadeva has how many servants? Millions and millions. So Kṛṣṇa is the root, these are His incarnations, and *jīvas* are Their servants. But there are those souls who are serving an incarnation, and those souls who are serving Kṛṣṇa directly. Why is Kṛṣṇa 'cheating' like this? The mood of Vraja is so beautiful, and the best of all *rasa* is *mādhurya-rasa*, so why doesn't He give *mādhurya-rasa* to everyone?

It is according to each soul's particular taste (*ruci*). To one *jīva* He may have only given liberation, and that soul will think, "He has been so merciful to me; there is nothing greater than this." Will Hanumān agree to become a father to Bhagavān and serve in that way? Never. And those who are serving Varāha Bhagavān are fully satisfied in that service. The servants of each and every incarnation consider His merciful touch to be the highest attainment. Gopa-kumāra saw that there were so many devotees in Nārāyaṇaloka, and they were all happy there. In Ayodhyā, Rāma is very merciful and affectionate to His devotees, but if Gopa-kumāra were to go to Ayodhyā, would he be happy? Would he even find cows in Ayodhyā? Yes, maybe in the home of a *brāhmaṇa* for the purpose of worship there may be a cow, but there will be no taking the cows out to graze as there is in Vṛndāvana. There, in all directions sacrifices are being performed with great pomp, and if a poor cowherd boy were to go there, he would be disturbed by all the smoke! Therefore he would not like it there under any condition. Nārada silently understood all these feelings within Gopa-kumāra's heart.

Chapter Ten

The Gradations in Service

Sometimes it happens that a *sādhaka* cannot understand his own heart. Just as a patient cannot identify his own disease, a *sādhaka*, due to his own weaknesses and shortcomings, cannot understand the nature of his own devotional sentiment. But a qualified doctor, by taking the pulse and seeing other symptoms, can understand those things which the patient himself cannot know. He will find the root cause of the disease. Where there is a fever, the doctor will not give any medicine for the fever itself, but instead he will give medicine for the cause of the fever. An ordinary man cannot act as such a doctor. Only someone with experience is the right person. Similarly, in our *bhajana* we may be unhappy – such misfortune may come to us. Those whose very life is *bhajana* can reveal to us what are our weaknesses and *anarthas* and from where they have arisen. They will give us a plan for eliminating those problems at the very root. They will say, "You must hear *hari-kathā*! And before hearing *hari-kathā*, you must serve the spiritual master with great faith." And if we respond, "But in trying to serve, my mind is very restless. How will I control it?", they will say, "Be confident – by the *guru*'s grace you will control it!"

The clever, intelligent *guru* understands the feelings in the heart of a disciple which even the disciple himself doesn't understand. Gopa-kumāra wants to ask, "Why is it that my heart is not satisfied here, even though I know that there is no greater place?" But due to shyness, he cannot ask.

Nārada, the crown jewel of spiritual doctors, recognised the symptoms, identified the disease and, without even inquiring anything from Gopa-kumāra, will give the answer. He will give different levels of answers, understanding that what Gopa-kumāra is saying may be irrelevant to the actual root cause of the disease itself. So he will tell him some things that are valuable for *sādhana*, and some things for *siddha*, the level of perfection. If we don't give the instructions that we hear from an experienced soul a place in our hearts and don't follow them, then not only in one or two births, but in countless millions of births we will not attain *hari-bhakti*. Understanding the inner feelings of Gopa-kumāra and knowing the reason for his unhappiness, Nārada is telling us how we should engage in *bhajana*. Therefore we must first prepare our minds to accept his line of thought. The defects that Nārada will point out to Gopa-kumāra are actually within us, and when we make a sincere effort to eliminate these defects, then we will really be engaging in *bhajana*. You can take it that real *bhajana* will be coming soon.

vaikuṇṭha-vāsino hy ete
kecid vai nitya-pārṣadāḥ
pare kṛṣṇasya kṛpayā
sādhayitvemam āgatāḥ

Bṛhad-bhāgavatāmṛta (2.4.194)

Some of the residents of Vaikuṇṭha are *nitya-siddha*, and some are *sādhana-siddha*. The *nitya-siddhas* are the eternal associates, and the *sādhana-siddhas* are those who came later, who by the mercy of Bhagavān attained perfection by the practice of *sādhana*. In the service of all devotees there is gradation. Some remain near to Bhagavān serving Him with the *cāmara*, while others are far away carrying out orders. For instance, Vasiṣṭha Ṛṣi is serving Rāmacandra in Ayodhyā, and his service is saying, "*maṅgalaṁ bhavatu*" and giving blessings. He gives advice for different things such as how to perform sacrifices and so on. Lakṣmaṇa also performs different services for Rāma. Once, when Rāma was away, Lakṣmaṇa sat with Niṣādarāja and sang the glories of Rāma for the entire night. In great happiness Niṣādarāja experienced ecstatic symptoms of love. Day and night Lakṣmaṇa serves Rāma, and Hanumān also serves Him, but when Sītā serves Him, then everyone else is sent outside, and they will all follow her order. In such services there is always gradation.

When trying to understand the reason for this gradation, one should not pass judgement by thinking, "This service is the highest, this service is lower." In Vaikuṇṭha all of the servants have their uniqueness. For example, cooking is being done there also. With great love, Rāma's mother Kauśalyā, Lakṣmaṇa's wife Urmilā and Sītā-devī are all cooking for Rāma. Are they considered mere cooks? No. Cooking is also *arcana*, so don't consider what is higher and lower in regard to *sevā*. To think "I am important" and that someone else is "just a cook" is *aparādha*. There is always gradation in service, but in all of it there is *prema*. Maybe in one particular form of *bhajana* there is more *prema*, and in another there is less, but when you arrive in Vaikuṇṭha, you'll find that everyone's service is extraordinary, and their *prema* is also extraordinary. We should understand this point. Therefore, there is no inferiority there, only gradation and speciality.

Hanumān, Jāmbavān, Sugrīva, Aṅgada and all others came together for the royal coronation of Rāmacandra. With great love Rāma had accepted all of their service and then began bidding them farewell. He called Sugrīva and placed a beautiful garland of jewels around his neck. Rāma embraced him and said, "I am indebted to you. If not for you, if you hadn't gone searching for Sītā, then we wouldn't have ultimately been victorious. Therefore remain in the kingdom and enjoy the fruits of your service. Sometimes I will call for you to come and see Me, or I will come to you Myself."

While Rāma was bidding them farewell, there were tears in the eyes of everyone. He called them one by one, and meeting with them, He gave cloth to some, to others He gave ornaments, and to others He gave something else. But where had Aṅgada hidden? Why had he hidden? He was thinking, "When He calls me, then I will have to go. But I don't want to leave Him!"

Rāma bid farewell to all, and Aṅgada remained hidden. Then Rāma said, "Where has Aṅgada gone?" He was hiding behind Hanumān, because he knew that Rāma wouldn't call Hanumān to bid him farewell. Rāma had called everyone else; so why didn't He call Hanumān? The reason was that in the home of Sugrīva there was a wife and there were children, so Rāma told Sugrīva, "Now you must return to them." Aṅgada had his mother, but Hanumān had left everything. All others had their objects of love, and together with that they had *bhakti* for Rāma also. Everyone had other points of affection, but Hanumān had no other point of affection. His only object of service was the feet of Rāma. He didn't even have his own hut! All others had their family, or their kingdom, or their building, or their position in society. Jāmbavān had his cave in Vindhyācala mountain, so Rāma told him, "Go, please... your wife is there." But if He said to Hanumān, "You go," then Hanumān would say, "My Lord, where will I go? I have not made a hut anywhere. You are my mother and my father also – You are my everything! Your feet are my only residence. I have nothing else besides You."

Rāmacandra saw that Hanumān was *akiñcana*, possessionless, whereas all the others were not. So as long as there is another point of affection besides Kṛṣṇa in our *bhajana*, then He will say, "All right, you go," and send us back to the place from which we have come. He sent back the wives of the *brāhmaṇas* who had their homes, husbands and children. But although some of the *gopīs* had husbands and even children, upon meeting Kṛṣṇa their attachment for them was washed away from their hearts forever. As long as we remain *akiñcana*, there will be no attachment to a mother or anyone else, and we will not be ordered to return.

bhajanānanda-sāmye 'pi
bhedaḥ kaścit prakalpyate
bāhyāntarīṇa-bhāvena
dūra-pārśva-sthatādinā

Bṛhad-bhāgavatāmṛta (2.4.195)

The *bhajanānanda*, the happiness derived from serving Bhagavān, is the same for all of His eternal associates, but some consider that there is a difference between serving Him from a position near to Him, and serving Him from a distance.

When a *kaniṣṭha-adhikārī* devotee engages in *bhajana*, he thinks, "There is no one like me. I am getting so much happiness from my *bhajana*. I am so impressive." Another man who is playing *mṛdaṅga* is thinking, "I am playing the *mṛdaṅga* in so many ways and a very beautiful melody is coming. I am playing so nicely." The *karatāla* player is also thinking in this way, and the man who is singing is feeling that there is great happiness in all of this. But when there will be some consideration of gradation, then we will understand that simply playing the *mṛdaṅga* and *karatālas* nicely does not constitute genuine *kīrtana*. Why do we play the *karatālas*? Day and night a party may be continuously playing golden, polished *karatālas* and *mṛdaṅgas* very, very nicely, while in another place there is one man alone, who without *mṛdaṅga* or *karatālas* is sitting and chanting:

gurudeva kṛpā-bindu diyā, kara' ei dāse
tṛṇāpekṣā ati hīna
sakala sahane, bala diyā kara'
nija-māne spṛhā-hīna

sakale sammāna, karite śakati
deha' nātha yathāyatha
tabe ta' gāiba, hari-nāma-sukhe
aparādha ha'be hata

Śaraṇāgati (*Bhajana-lālasā* 11)

> O Gurudeva, please give this servant of yours a drop of your mercy, which will make him realise that he is more insignificant than a piece of straw. Give me the strength to tolerate all difficulties, and please make me devoid of all desires for personal prestige. Only when you have given me the ability to properly respect all living beings will all my offences cease, and I will be able to sing the holy name in great happiness.

With great feeling he is singing it, with his bodily limbs shivering and tears flowing from his eyes. So between the happiness of all those *mṛdaṅga* and *karatāla* players and that of the one lone man performing *kīrtana* with such feeling, will there be some distinction? Very much so. The lone man's chanting is really *kīrtana*. And that '*kīrtana*' that has very beautiful *mṛdaṅga* notes, a beautiful melody, and has everyone involved in it, but is devoid of even a little genuine devotion, is something else entirely. Therefore in *kīrtana*, sincere sentiment is necessary, and just as in *bhajana* there is gradation, in *arcana* there is also gradation. One man is offering *arcana* with a pure sentiment, one man is offering *arcana* without any such sentiment, and another man who blasphemes Vaiṣṇavas is also offering *arcana* to the deity. Will it all be equal? No.

In the spiritual realm also there is gradation in the service of the eternal associates of Bhagavān. Just as one servant brings flowers, another makes a garland, another hands the garland to Lakṣmī-devī, another prepares food and another offers it. In this way there is gradation. One is serving near to Him, and others are serving from farther away. If the one who is serving near to Him thinks that those who are serving from farther away are inferior, he is mistaken. The *bhāva*, or sentiment, is the important thing.

Caitanya Mahāprabhu's servant Govinda dāsa may think that Svarūpa Dāmodara and Rāya Rāmānanda are only servants who remain at a distance from the Lord, and who only come for a few minutes or an hour and make Mahāprabhu cry. Govinda dāsa himself wipes away the tears of Mahāprabhu, and then they come and make Him cry again. So he may think, "Why do they have to come and make Him cry again?"

Govinda dāsa is always saying to the Lord, "Prabhu, please don't cry." Then Svarūpa Dāmodara will come and make Him cry again, so what will Govinda dāsa think? Therefore it is not that the servant who is nearer is necessarily better. In this case the servants that remained farther away from Mahāprabhu are higher. It is not a question of the physical proximity or distance, but of the heart's nearness to or distance from Him. That service to Hari, Guru and the Vaiṣṇavas in which there is the most love is the best.

When the four Kumāras arrived at Vaikuṇṭha, the gatekeepers there, Jaya and Vijaya, raised their sticks and said, "You cannot enter!" Thinking that they were the masters there, they prohibited the four Kumāras from entering. Should those doormen have thought that since the Kumāras had come from a long distance they couldn't have known that it was the time that the Lord takes rest? The Kumāras knew everything. They came in humility with folded hands, but they knew everything. Jaya and Vijaya didn't understand the feelings and the *prema* that the Kumāras have for Bhagavān. Is it like this only sometimes? Most of the time it is like this! One who is serving near to the Lord or near to the spiritual master cannot understand the devotional sentiment of those who are serving at a distance. Therefore we should be careful not to think so highly of ourselves and we should always remember the 'misfortune' that came upon Jaya and Vijaya. We should understand how to behave properly and avoid being arrogant.

Generally these things are said for those practising *sādhana*, but even in the state of perfection this can happen. This incident occurred in Vaikuṇṭha, but it is for giving instruction to those of us performing *sādhana*. In any situation we should never have a mood of disrespect towards Vaiṣṇavas, nor should we ever speak ill of them.

Kṛṣṇa has so many eternal associates, and they all have their uniqueness. There are so many incarnations and sources of incarnations of Bhagavān, and They all have Their associates, but Kṛṣṇa's associates are more special than them, more special than the devotees of Nṛsiṁha and all other incarnations. The devotees of other incarnations serve their Lord with humility and folded hands, but Kṛṣṇa's devotees sometimes fight and quarrel with Him and display *māna*, jealous anger. Such a *bhāva* is found in their service, and therefore they are greater.

vadanti kecid bhagavān hi kṛṣṇaḥ
su-sac-cid-ānanda-ghanaika-mūrtiḥ
sa yat paraṁ brahma pare tu sarve
tat-pārṣadā brahmamayā vimuktāḥ

Bṛhad-bhāgavatāmṛta (2.4.200)

Some say that Kṛṣṇa and His many incarnations are all one in *tattva*, although there is some gradation and speciality in *rasa* and manifestation of potency. That is all right. In Their associates there is the same uniqueness, but will we take it that some of these associates are inferior? Don't think in this way. Whether they are *nitya-siddha* or *sādhana-siddha* devotees, it says here that they are all fully, eternally liberated.

Some say that Kṛṣṇa is *parabrahma*, the supreme spiritual entity, and that all of His eternal associates are *brahma*, spirit. In some places it has been stated like this, and this is also not incorrect. What is *brahmānanda*? The inherent blissfulness (*ānanda*) of the living entity is called *brahmānanda*. The *jīva* has been called *brahma*, but the *jīva* has not been referred to as *parabrahma*; *parabrahma* is Kṛṣṇa. We don't consider that *brahma* and *parabrahma* are one and put them in the same class. We consider the *jīva* to be the servant: *dāso 'smi dāso 'smi*. The scriptures say "*brahma evaṁ bhavati* – one certainly becomes *brahma*", in the Gītā there is "*viśate tad anantaram* – one then enters into that", and there are also similar verses in *Śrīmad-Bhāgavatam*. In Purī, Sārvabhauma Bhaṭṭācārya came to have hatred for the theory of monism (*brahmavāda*), but not all liberation is worthy of hatred. *Mukti* can also mean attaining service at the feet of Bhagavān. But Sārvabhauma despised the word *mukti*, and he also despised referring to the *jīva* as *brahma*.

Hearing this line of thought, Gopa-kumāra asked Nārada a question:

pṛṣṭaṁ mayedaṁ bhagavan dharā-tale
tiṣṭhanti yāḥ śrī-pratimā mahā-prabhoḥ
tāḥ sac-cid-ānanda-ghanās tvayā matā
nīlādri-nāthaḥ puruṣottamo yathā

eko 'pi bhagavān sāndra-
sac-cid-ānanda-vigrahaḥ
kṛpayā tatra tatrāste
tat-tad-rūpeṇa līlayā

Bṛhad-bhāgavatāmṛta (2.4.202–3)

In this world, there are many deities of Bhagavān. In Purī there are Jagannātha, Baladeva and Subhadrā, in Śrī Raṅgam there is Raṅganātha, and in those places They are being worshipped. There, whether the *prasāda* is cooked or uncooked, its acceptability is not considered. Those deities are established there to mercifully give *darśana* to the people of this world. Gopa-kumāra asked, "There are so many forms of Bhagavān in this world, like Jagannātha and Raṅganātha, and many other deities. In what way should we respect Them? Are They all solidified forms of *sac-cid-ānanda*? By offering *pūjā* to any of Them, will it be considered offering *pūjā* to Bhagavān?"

There are so many deities in this world, and all are *sac-cid-ānanda*. For showing mercy to the devotees, the one Bhagavān is situated in many different forms as His pastime. But we are not able to serve Him directly. If we try to serve Him just as Lakṣmī-devī is serving Nārāyaṇa, as the *gopīs* are serving Kṛṣṇa, and as Prahlāda Mahārāja is serving Nṛsiṁhadeva, at some point we will say, "O Lord, the time to take rest has long passed. Half the night I have remained without sleep. I am feeling very sleepy." So Bhagavān will say, "Then you go and sleep," and we will have to go and take rest. If the deity were to speak and express His desire – "Massage My feet. This food has not been prepared properly; make it like this" – we would become easily discouraged.

We want to serve according to our own desire. If we have not even served according to the desire of our *guru* – if we could not follow him properly – then how will we serve Bhagavān directly? If we are placed directly in front of Bhagavān and He says, "Do this service for Me!", can we do it? Could we do anything and everything He asked of us at any time? We are not able to. Therefore the deity remains silent. However much service we offer, He just remains silent. So Bhagavān has assumed all these forms for giving mercy to the devotees. He understands that by no other means will we be able to serve Him in our conditioned state, so He becomes the deity form, remains silent, and in the end He just accepts our obeisances. For this reason He has manifested these deities.

There are many different types of *ruci* in the living entities, so to accept service from them according to their *ruci*, He has assumed different forms. Some will serve in *dāsya-rasa*, some in *sakhya* and some in *vātsalya*. Why has Kṛṣṇa become Laḍḍū-Gopāla? Because then many people can worship Him as their son. When women become old and their offspring have all grown up, they still desire to render the service of a parent. Women are so inclined towards serving children that not only will they forget about serving their husbands, they will even engage the husband in the service of the children! The wife will say to her husband, "Help me a little with the children. Catch that child! Bring some milk for the children. The children are sick, call the doctor for them. Take the children to school!" The sentiment of serving children is *vātsalya-bhāva*, so for them Kṛṣṇa has become Bāla-Gopāla, for others He becomes something else, but all these deities are eternal. To accept service Kṛṣṇa has become the deity and assumed many forms; and He doesn't speak. If He spoke, then we couldn't serve Him. At one, two, or three o'clock in the night He may feel cold and require some service when His servant is in deep sleep. So what would happen if He always expressed His desire? Therefore He remains silent and accepts our service.

But if we suppose that He says nothing because He knows nothing, that is an offence. He doesn't speak or move, but we should understand that He sees everything. He knows the true scope of what we do, and we must accept the reaction to whatever we do. Therefore in front of the deity we shouldn't spread our legs, talk too much, become angry at anyone, or inordinately display affection for anyone. Before the deity don't offer obeisances to anyone, and don't speak too loudly. All these things should be given careful attention. If in the deity's room there is fighting and arguing, and the *pujārī* goes to do the *pūjā* with an agitated mind, that will be an offence. With a disturbed mind we should not do the deity's *pūjā*. But He remains silent anyway. We take it that He sees nothing, but He is very merciful and sometimes doesn't even accept the offences of His devotees.

Those who leave other types of *sādhana* to perform *arcana* of the deity will benefit. But Gopa-kumāra is saying to Nārada, the very founder of *pūjā*, "Prabhu, in some places in the scriptures it is written that there are some who are offering *arcana* to the deity, but are disrespecting devotees."

arcāyām eva haraye
pūjāṁ yaḥ śraddhayehate
na tad-bhakteṣu cānyeṣu
sa bhaktaḥ prākṛtaḥ smṛtaḥ

Śrīmad-Bhāgavatam (11.2.47)

A devotee who worships the deity in the temple with faith but does not properly respect other devotees or people in general is called a materialistic devotee, and is included within the lowest class of devotees.

yo māṁ sarveṣu bhūteṣu
santam ātmānam īśvaram
hitvārcāṁ bhajate mauḍhyād
bhasmany eva juhoti saḥ

Śrīmad-Bhāgavatam (3.29.22)

One who worships the deity in the temple but does not know that Bhagavān in the form of the Supersoul is situated in every living entity's heart is in ignorance, and is compared to one who offers oblations of ghee onto ashes.

Kṛṣṇa is situated within each and every *jīva*. There is no soul where there is not Bhagavān. Yet in many scriptures such as Nārada's own *bhakti-sūtra*, the *Nārada-pañcarātra*, it is stated that there are people who worship the deity in the temple, but insult and disrespect other living entities and even blaspheme Vaiṣṇavas as they are carrying on their *pūjā*. Apparently they are very strict: if a mango has mistakenly been put in an unclean place, or if someone has seen it and desired to taste it, then they will throw that mango away and it won't be offered to the deity. At the time of cooking they cover their faces with cloth, and at the time of kneading dough there will be no speaking. They honour all of these principles, but they disrespect devotees. They pass judgement on whether devotees are higher or lower, and thus it is written that the *arcana* that these people are offering to the deity is like the pouring of ghee onto ashes. And furthermore:

aham uccāvacair dravyaiḥ
kriyayotpannayānaghe
naiva tuṣye 'rcito 'rcāyāṁ
bhūta-grāmāvamāninaḥ

Śrīmad-Bhāgavatam (3.29.24)

[Kapiladeva said:] O sinless mother, even if someone worships the deity with all the proper rituals and various kinds of paraphernalia, I am never pleased by a person who is ignorant of My presence in all living entities.

All souls are the residence of Bhagavān. Especially here this instruction is being spoken for devotees. Those who perform exclusive *bhajana* of Bhagavān must not insult any living entity. We are insulting others, but so nicely we are performing *arcana*. Even if we are giving all respect to Vaiṣṇavas, still Bhagavān will not be satisfied; there will still be offences because respect is not being given to all souls. *Pratimā-manda-buddhīnām*: those of small intelligence are offering this type of *arcana-pūjā*. In another place it is also said:

arcye viṣṇau śilā-dhīr guruṣu nara-matir-vaiṣṇave jāti-buddhir
viṣṇor vā vaiṣṇavānāṁ kali-mala-mathane pāda-tīrthe 'mbu-buddhiḥ

There are those who consider that Bhagavān is in the deity. Yes, inside different things there is gradation in the degree of Bhagavān's presence, but they don't consider that the *śilā* is Bhagavān Himself. They also think that the Lord's *caraṇāmṛta*, which dispels the influence of Kali-yuga, is ordinary water. And they further consider that the object of *arcana*, the deity, is sometimes composed of 'second-number' marble, whereas in another place there is a deity composed of first-class marble. They consider, "Oh, this deity at Govardhana is very beautiful, but the deities we see in the temples of Vṛndāvana are not this beautiful. Here, Kṛṣṇa's nose is a little straighter, His eyes are a little longer, and this is very good." Bhagavān does not accept *pūjā* from people who think like this.

They also consider the dust of the feet of Vaiṣṇavas to be ordinary dust, and the foot-water of the Vaiṣṇavas to be ordinary water. They have faith in the holy places and the water there, but in the *caraṇāmṛta* of Vaiṣṇavas they don't have the same faith. They place their faith in the skin and blood of the material body, which is destined to perish. The soul is inside every type of body, but they don't understand that the *ātmā* is a dear part of Bhagavān. It doesn't matter that the soul is bound within a material body; its intrinsic form is as a servant of Bhagavān. Therefore it should be respected. Respect is given on different levels, so we should give appropriate respect to all others. And what is the position of he who doesn't do this? *Sa eva go-kharaḥ* (*Śrīmad- Bhāgavatam* 10.84.13). *Go* means 'animal' and *kharaḥ* means 'donkey'. Don't take it that here *go* means 'cow' – the cow is a very pure thing! It means such a person is no better than an animal, and the most foolish of the animals is the donkey.

Gopa-kumāra is asking Nārada, "Prabhu, why has this been stated in the scriptures? Please explain this. Some of the deity worshippers have been referred to like this, but you said that those who perform *arcana* are the most fortunate. How can this be reconciled?"

An ordinary person cannot reconcile it, and even a lower-level *madhyama-adhikārī* devotee cannot reconcile it. Only an intermediate or higher-level *madhyama-adhikārī* who is conversant with the scriptures and who has attained the mercy of the spiritual master can grasp all of this. And because Nārada is the original founder of the path of *pūjā* and also the foremost preacher of that path, who could possibly know this science better than him?

Chapter Eleven

The Proper Mood for Arcana

Upon hearing Gopa-kumāra's question concerning *arcana-pūjā*, Nārada was overwhelmed with supreme happiness and immediately embraced him. Why did he embrace him? Because in regard to this subject there is some doubt in us. If someone asks us, "Okay, is this deity made from real marble, or false marble? Is it made from pure metals, or alloys?" will we be pleased and embrace that person? Rather we will be thinking, "Seeing this person is sinful." But in Vaikuṇṭha, it is not possible to have such doubts. In Vaikuṇṭha this outlook cannot come, so there is no personal necessity in Gopa-kumāra's asking. He is asking for the benefit of those of us on the path of *sādhana*. He has no doubt himself, but doubt remains in us. Therefore, for our welfare he has asked. Nārada saw that he cares so much for others that he is asking this question. Being very pleased, he embraced Gopa-kumāra and slowly answered him.

Nārada said, "The deity is directly Bhagavān Himself. The Raṅganātha deity, the deity of Pandharpura (in Maharastra), the Veṅkateśvara deity, Jagannātha in Purī, the deities of Māyāpura and the *śrī vigrahas* of Vṛndāvana – Govinda, Gopīnātha and Madana-mohana – are all directly Bhagavān. Sometimes the deity says, 'On the side of My nose there is a small hole; place an ornament there. And after feeding Me, take Me out. I never go anywhere.' And His devotee thinks, 'He cannot speak or move! Why is He speaking? And if He can speak, then certainly He can move also, so I need not worry.' Such pastimes are performed by the deity. Sometimes He asks for an ornament, and sometimes during the night He comes to a devotee in a dream and speaks with him. The devotees in Purī perform *kīrtana* from the *Gīta-govinda*, and when the deity wants to join them, He races off the altar, tearing His clothing and breaking His ornaments on the way. Are such activities ordinary? Therefore one must abandon any mundane conception of the deity. He is directly Bhagavān Himself.

"Besides this, what is the consideration that 'this is an old deity,' or 'this is a new one,' or 'this is one we made ourselves'? Girirāja is brought from Govardhana, or a *śālagrāma-śilā* is brought from somewhere, and we worship Him in that form. Or in our home with metal or some other elements we have made a *mūrti*, and by worshipping that *mūrti* we feel great happiness in our hearts. If anyone abandons his *varṇāśrama-dharma* responsibilities to perform *pūjā* of Bhagavān with great faith, there is no fault in it. We must abandon the mundane conception of the deity, as He is the direct form of Bhagavān."

No one made Baṅke-bihārī; He appeared by Himself. Others were manifest by devotees: Madana-mohana was manifest by Sanātana Gosvāmī, Govindajī and Dāmodara were manifest by Rūpa Gosvāmī, and Gopīnātha was manifest by Madhu Paṇḍita. All of these deities appeared by Themselves or were installed by great devotees, so concerning Them there is no doubt. But by sincerely serving other deities that you have brought from somewhere and have established yourself with *mantra* and *abhiṣeka*, you will also attain the topmost *bhakti*. In this method there is no fault whatsoever:

na pātityādi-doṣaḥ syād
guṇa eva mahān mataḥ
sevottamā matā bhaktiḥ
phalaṁ yā paramaṁ mahat

Bṛhad-bhāgavatāmṛta (2.4.209)

There is a great quality in *pūjā*: from this service one will obtain a great result, the topmost *bhakti*. If anyone leaves his *varṇāśrama-dharma* responsibilities to engage in *pūjā* with the aim of attaining *bhagavad-bhakti*, and has genuinely entered into *bhajana*, but in this birth he has not attained perfection because for some reason in the midst of performing *bhajana* his *bhakti* has stopped – for whatever reason – then what is the loss? And if that person remains within *varṇāśrama-dharma* for his entire life but doesn't perform *bhajana* or serve Bhagavān, then what will he have gained? All of his life within *varṇāśrama* he served his parents, served his family *gurus*, gave charity and alms, bathed at holy places and everything, but he didn't engage in *bhajana*. So then what did he gain? Mahārāja Hariścandra[4] received the association of great personalities like Viśvāmitra and became a great devotee; therefore he was benefited. Otherwise there would have been no benefit resulting from all of his *dharma*.

If someone in an immature stage left his vow of celibacy (*brahmacarya*) and for some reason didn't reach perfection, then there is no loss for him. Why? Because in his next birth he will begin again from the point of his attainment and then go on to success. It is just as when we study in a school, pass the courses, and then go to another school and study further.

If anyone takes up *bhajana*, offering *pūjā* to the deity, and chanting the holy name, then all connections with the world and *varṇāśrama* are broken. This is called *kriyālopa*, absence of activity. Ordinarily, those who have left their worldly duties would have to appoint millions of great sages to perform all the ceremonies necessary for atonement in order to rectify their mistake. But those who have entered into *bhajana* will not have to undergo any atonement. Any man who leaves his worldly duties for selfish

---

4 The story of Hariścandra Mahārāja is found in *Śrīmad-Bhāgavatam*, Ninth Canto, Chapter Seven.

motives has five debts upon him: to the demigods, the sages, the forefathers, the family members and to all other living entities.

What is the duty of a son? How will he fulfil his debt to his forefathers? Just as his father raised him and made him qualified to live in the world, then he must also marry, have offspring and make them qualified to live in the world. Then his debt to his forefathers is completed. But without marrying it can't be done. And how will a girl fulfil her debt? By serving just as her mother did. Her mother brought her up and looked after her, and like that she will serve her husband, give birth to children, raise them to maturity, and then she will be free of her debt. The debt to the demigods is like this also, as are all other debts. As long as one's wife has not said, "Go then! Go and do *bhajana*," one cannot leave household life to take up *bhajana*.

Yet in a very discreet way Mahāprabhu disregarded the injunctions of the scriptures and left home. He left behind His elderly mother, made no arrangements for her needs, and giving up all responsibilities, He left. He disregarded the injunctions of the scriptures, but for what? For the service of Govinda. So when someone leaves in this way, it is called *kriyālopa*.

According to the injunctions, first one should be a *brahmacārī*, then a *gṛhastha*, then a *vānaprastha* and finally a *sannyāsī*. But some go straight from *brahmacārī* to *sannyāsa* without following *gṛhastha-dharma*, so the debt to their forefathers is upon them. However, there will be no necessity of atonement for this if one has left to take up the *bhajana* of Mukunda. But it is said that those who have resorted to *kriyālopa* for some purpose other than engaging in *bhagavad-bhajana* must appoint three million *brāhmaṇas* to perform ceremonies for their atonement – the kind of *brāhmaṇas* with long beards and their hair tied high on their heads who live only on milk. Day and night they will be chanting "*oṁ svāhā, oṁ svāhā*". Those who need atonement must appoint them, and if they don't follow this process of atonement, Bhagavān will punish them. But for devotees who have left their worldly responsibilities to take up *bhajana*, this atonement is not necessary.

There are also sixty-four kinds of *bhakti*, and if someone becomes absorbed in one kind and is unable to do the rest, for this also there is no need of atonement. But be especially careful of one thing: while absorbed in worshipping the deity or chanting the holy name, do not offend any *uttama* Vaiṣṇava. Always be careful of this. Other things Kṛṣṇa will tolerate, but this He will not tolerate.

tāvat karmāṇi kurvīta
na nirvidyeta yāvatā
mat-kathā-śravaṇādau vā
śraddhā yāvan na jāyate

Śrīmad-Bhāgavatam (11.20.9)

One needs to follow the path of *karma-kāṇḍa* only as long as he has no renunciation. At the time when renunciation comes, and he understands that worldly attachments are a source of misery, and that "I am a spirit soul", he will no longer need to follow the path of *karma*. Then he can go along the path of *jñāna*. Beyond this, if by *śravaṇa, kīrtana, smaraṇa, pāda-sevana* or any other way *bhakti* comes, then also there is no need to follow the path of *karma*.

For example, Rabindranatha Tagore never studied in school, nor did he go to college. He was taught at home. First his parents taught him, and after this a tutor came and taught him. The acquisition from his previous lives was such that automatically he became highly learned. For him studying in schools was not necessary. Similarly, those who have given their hearts to hearing and chanting about Kṛṣṇa have no need to follow the path of *karma*. They may perform some karmic activity, but it will only be for the benefit of others. It will not be for themselves. But wherever there is some faith in *bhakti*, no *karma* is necessary. For performing karmic activities properly, there are many books like *Manu-smṛti*, *Artha-saṁhitā*, the writings of *Yājñavalkya*, etc., and in society there are so many conventions for that purpose. These things are not for those who have entered into *bhajana*. If *sādhakas* do them, it is all right, and if they don't do them, there is no harm.

Some people read the *Gītā* verse *sarva-dharmān parityajya, mām ekaṁ śaraṇaṁ vraja* and they take it to mean, "Leaving aside all material attachments, follow the path of *karma* and come to My shelter." But what did our *gosvāmīs* say? Leave all attachments and also the path of *karma*, just as all of our previous *ācāryas* did, and as so many devotees have done. Being a soul surrendered unto the Lord, Raghunātha dāsa Gosvāmī left his home. Did he engage in any *karma-kāṇḍa* activities? Not knowing *bhakti-rasa*, those of meagre intelligence follow the path of *karma*, but for those who understand the true nature of *bhakti*, there is no prescription for such activity. They are above karmic activity and atonement. The Lord Himself sometimes performs certain *karma-kāṇḍa* functions for the benefit of the world, and saints and devotees also do it, but only for the welfare of this world.

yad yad ācarati śreṣṭhas
tat tad evetaro janaḥ
sa yat pramāṇaṁ kurute
lokas tad anuvartate

Bhagavad-gītā (3.21)

Common men imitate the actions of great men. Everyone follows the standards which great personalities establish.

What is *karma*? When we do anything with a selfish aim and taste the fruit of our own activities, it is *karma* and we become implicated in its reaction. For instance, "I am offering *arcana* to my deity, and as a result, everyone will praise me and I will make so much money."

That *pūjā* will simply be *karma*. That which is done for Bhagavān is *bhakti*, and that which is done for liberation is *jñāna*. Bhagavān will accept *pūjā* offered with the aim of pleasing Him.

If we are thinking, "Bhagavān will be pleased by my service, and therefore He will give me a wife, husband, son, daughter or money," then that is *karma*. But from those who are offering *pūjā* solely for the pleasure of Bhagavān – even though there may be some mistake in it – it will be accepted as genuine *bhakti*.

Next Nārada spoke this verse:

siddhiḥ syād bhagavad-dṛṣṭyā
tṛṇa-sammānanād api
sakṛd-uccaraṇān nāmā-
bhāsasya śravaṇāt tathā

Bṛhad-bhāgavatāmṛta (2.4.210)

If with *bhagavad-buddhi*, awareness of Bhagavān's presence, one offers obeisances even to a piece of straw, or offers something to that straw with great feeling and shows it respect, then this action will be the fulfiller of desires and the giver of perfection. And remembering the name of his son, Ajāmila unknowingly achieved a spiritual destination. Yes, unknowingly. If we have given one of our family members the name of a *rādhā-dāsī* or the name of a *kṛṣṇa-dāsa*, such as Madana-mohana, will there be any result from that? Certainly there will be benefit, even though calling out the Lord's name in this way is *ābhāsa*, a semblance of pure chanting. In this way Nārada has said that with *bhagavad-buddhi* anyone can offer respect even to a piece of straw. Why? Because in this world there is nothing that isn't related to Bhagavān. Is there anything? No, all objects are the abode of Bhagavān.

If we see that Bhagavān is even within a donkey, then because of this vision will we have to take birth as a donkey? No, it isn't like that. It is written somewhere that *tilaka* was applied to a donkey, and *tulasī* neck beads placed around his neck. The people were saying that if one didn't offer *praṇāma* to the donkey, then that person wouldn't obtain *bhakti*. So someone was devoutly offering *praṇāma* to the donkey. Yes, if one does this with the vision that Bhagavān is in all things, there is no harm, but thinking that this donkey is Bhagavān – that is polluted intelligence. Prahlāda Mahārāja offered *praṇāma* to everything – birds, animals, insects, straw – why? Because he understood that without the presence of Bhagavān, nothing can exist; not because "This is Bhagavān Himself."

If we were to see a peacock feather that has fallen in the dust and been trodden on by others, what would we do? At once we would pick it up and clean it off, touch it to our head, and keep it in some pure place. Why would we keep it – because "this is Kṛṣṇa"? No, because this thing is dear to Kṛṣṇa; Kṛṣṇa wears it. This is *bhagavad-buddhi*. If with this outlook one offers respect to a piece of straw, that will be greatly helpful in attaining *bhagavad-bhakti*. So what to speak of our progress if we offer respect directly to the deity of Bhagavān?

Non-moving living entities, and all things, are manifestations of the *śakti* of Bhagavān, and there is no harm in offering them obeisances, just as Prahlāda Mahārāja did. Everything is part of Bhagavān; we should understand that. If we can attain perfection even by seeing straw and other unimportant objects with the vision of *bhagavad-buddhi*, then how much quicker will the result come if we are directly remembering the *śrī vigraha*? If we worship a deity in the temple, or if we establish a deity in our home with a fire sacrifice, *abhiṣeka* and Vedic *mantra*, then how can there be any fault in this? There is certainly no fault in it. Therefore deity worship has been written about in all scriptures, and now Nārada will explain why certain statements are found regarding particular faults in *pūjā*:

kadāpi kṛṣṇa-pratimārcanavatāṁ
na sambhavet kṛṣṇa-pareṣv anādaraḥ

ghaṭeta cet karhy api tad-viṣaktito
gṛṇanti nāgas tad amī stuvanty atha
Bṛhad-bhāgavatāmṛta (2.4.212)

If anyone is really a devotee – even a *kaniṣṭha-adhikārī* who may not even know *tattva* but is sincerely engaged in *pūjā* of the deity – then it will not be possible for him to disrespect any Vaiṣṇava. A materialistic devotee is still a devotee, isn't he? But he will never be able to show any disrespect. Upon seeing a Vaiṣṇava he will offer *praṇāma* and say, "Please take *darśana* of our Ṭhākurajī. Please take His *prasāda*," and he will do nothing more. If someone does disrespect a Vaiṣṇava, then he has not yet even become a *kaniṣṭha* devotee. Nārada is saying that if a devotee is really doing *arcana*, then he will not be able to disrespect any Vaiṣṇava. Not even a new devotee can do it.

One such opportunity came. A devotee was seated to begin his *arcana*, and then an elder Vaiṣṇava came. The *pujārī* was not immediately able to show that Vaiṣṇava respect. In such a situation Vaiṣṇavas are very merciful. They will say, "No, no – do your service, you should do your *pūjā*." The *pujārī* didn't know that the Vaiṣṇava had come because he was absorbed in his *arcana*. Then that Vaiṣṇava was even more merciful towards him and didn't consider that there was any fault. If that Vaiṣṇava who came had considered this to be an *aparādha* on the part of the *pujārī*, then he would not have been a Vaiṣṇava at all. But at the same time, there can be the possibility of *aparādha* here. Once Baladeva arrived in an assembly and Romaharṣana knowingly did not get up and offer *praṇāma*. He was not absorbed in anything at the time, and he was thinking, "I am worshipful to everyone." So he didn't show respect, and Baladeva finished him.

If a devotee is absorbed in *pūjā* or offering prayers and a Vaiṣṇava comes, but the devotee does not see the Vaiṣṇava due to being absorbed in his prayer, the Vaiṣṇava will take their error as a great quality. They won't take it as an offence. But if one knows that a Vaiṣṇava has come and intentionally neglects him, thinking that the Vaiṣṇava is insignificant, that will be an offence. Then the deity will not accept that person's *pūjā*.

Suppose we spend a great sum of money for a festival for the deity and we are busy making the arrangements for one whole month. We make elaborate arrangements for the distribution of *prasāda* to the thousands of people who come. We put up electric decorations and make elaborate arrangements for the *pūjā*, but if behind it is a desire for prestige, that *pūjā* will be useless and the deity will not accept it. If we do this so that our prestige in the world will increase and so that people will praise us, then the deity will not accept our *pūjā*.

If someone offers just a little simple *pūjā* that is genuinely for the pleasure of Kṛṣṇa, then He accepts it; but when there are impure motives in the *pūjā*, He will not accept it. Therefore at the time of offering *pūjā* we must have the proper sentiment in our hearts, and also at the time of taking His name. Sometimes we may say to someone, "Hey you, come here!" If we call Kṛṣṇa in the same way, will He listen? If we call Him and the correct feelings are not there, He will not listen. We may say to someone nicely and with some feeling, "Please come and take *prasāda*." If we approach Bhagavān in that mood, He will come. Otherwise, if seeing that an offering is late we rush through it by quickly chanting *oṁ kṛṣṇāya namaḥ*, will He come? Only when there is sincere desire from within will Bhagavān accept an offering. Otherwise, He will not be hungry and will not accept it. We should consider these things in whichever limb of *bhakti* we are engaged in. If we are preparing food but we have no genuine desire to please Him, we are not in the proper mood, then the deity won't accept any of it, because He has no need. He is hungry only for *prema*. Taking all of these things into consideration, we should engage in *kīrtana*, *śravana*, *smaraṇa*, *vandana* and everything with *prema*. Then Bhagavān will certainly accept what has been offered.

One may be singing *kīrtana* in a sweet melody, and some great musicians are there. They know all the rhythms and classical melodies and are playing them very sweetly, and this attracts the minds of many people. But unless it is exclusively for the pleasure of Bhagavān, then the only result from this *kīrtana* is that those who are listening are enjoying it. Those who are seated there and playing the *kīrtana* will get no benefit if it is not really for His satisfaction. This, then, is not an easy thing; when all of one's activities are done solely for Bhagavān's satisfaction, it is called *śuddha-bhakti*, unalloyed devotion.

These days we can see how degraded things have become as we enter further into the age of Kali. Some people take the property of the deity to be their own, and in their *pūjā* they think, "I am important" and "I am the master." For this reason there is then sometimes a court case, and such persons go on quarrelling and fighting, sometimes even up to spilling blood and killing each other rather than turning the service over to someone who may be more qualified. Inside them is aggression towards other living entities. They have more money, more influence, more disciples, and by any means their opulence has increased, but they continue to disrespect other devotees. Such people will certainly be deprived of what the scriptures declare to be the results of *pūjā*: love for Bhagavān, *darśana* of Bhagavān, and ultimately attaining Vaikuṇṭha.

Once, Nārada said to Bhagavān, "My Lord, I see that many people don't respect devotees. Why is it like this? They should respect devotees."

Bhagavān replied, "What to speak of devotees, they don't even respect Me!" And desiring to prove the point, He said, "I will show you something. Tomorrow there will be a very big *bhaṇḍāra* (an arrangement for distributing free *prasāda* to *sādhus*). I will go to that *bhaṇḍāra* personally, and you will see how they respect Me there."

Bhagavān went to the *bhaṇḍāra*. It was a very big programme, and those who were invited had been sent tickets. All of the important people with tickets had entered, and then one old man with a black complexion who was so thin that it appeared as if his back and stomach were touching, came begging. "Please let me enter. I haven't eaten for four days," he said. He tried to enter a little inside, but was stopped by the guard. "Do you have a ticket? No?"

In the end the old man pushed the guard aside and entered. The guard became angry and notified the supervisor, but the man didn't care; pushing his way in, he took a leaf for a plate and went and sat down at the back. Then the supervisor approached him and said, "Where is your ticket? You are not honouring this? Grab this man and throw him out."

When the beggar didn't get up, four or five men forcefully ejected him and slammed the door behind him. Meanwhile, Nārada was watching. "O Lord, I see now: despite all Your efforts – pushing Your way in, taking a leaf and sitting in the back – after quarrelling with You, they ejected You!"

So we shouldn't show such disrespect to others. We should all be careful. If someone comes to our home or temple, we should certainly give him something – it might be Him! And He may even come in the form of a *māyāvādī*. We should give him something and show him some respect also; otherwise it will constitute aggression towards another. If a *sādhu* comes, then show him some respect. Knowing Bhagavān to be inside everyone, give him respect and speak to him with sweet words. *Bhagavad-bhakti* is established on a foundation of very beautiful philosophy, and if we don't honour these things, fault will come upon us. We should serve the deity with the correct vision and offer respect to all accordingly. When Gopa-kumāra went to Prayaga, he saw different kinds of sacrifice going on there, and everyone – even the crows and monkeys – was given *prasāda*.

Nārada uses the word *aviduṣa*. *Viduṣa* means a scholar, and *aviduṣa* means one who knows nothing, a fool. From a foolish person Bhagavān doesn't accept *pūjā*. But if someone has no knowledge but is faithful, from that person He will accept *pūjā*. Here, *viduṣa* and *aviduṣa* do not refer to whether one has studied the Vedas or not. Though having studied the Vedas and other scriptures, one can still be a fool. If after having read the *Gītā*, *Bhāgavatam*, *Rāmāyaṇa* and all the Purāṇas one still has no faith in the deity, he is simply a fool.

One day a devotee who came to our temple sat looking at the deities for half an hour. We were wondering if he was experiencing some great sentiment or what he was thinking. After gazing at the deities for so long, he called someone over and said, "From where has this *mūrti* come? There is a defect in it." This is *aviduṣa*, even though this man had been a member of our order for at least forty or fifty years.

Those that are *aviduṣa* don't give proper respect to anyone – not to Vaiṣṇavas, and not to others. Bhagavān doesn't accept *pūjā* from such people, but He will accept *pūjā* from those who are ignorant but innocent, because they are not offensive. In *arcana*, what comes first? Offering *bhoga*. After that? The ghee lamp. Then? Bathing water in a conchshell, followed by cloths, followed by *caraṇāmṛta*, and after this the *cāmara*. So if someone accidentally changes the sequence of these things and offers the *cāmara* at the wrong time, will the deity reject his *pūjā*? This *pūjā* He will accept. But those who do their *pūjā* with sixteen ingredients but no faith, just so that people will come and give money – where the *pujārī* is thinking that he made thirty rupees this week and he will make another thirty rupees next week – are committing *aparādha*. Bhagavān won't accept *pūjā* from those people. But from those who are ignorant yet innocent He will always accept *pūjā*, even from a person with selfish desires (*sakāma*). If a *sakāma* person is faithful, then after a long time Bhagavān will still give him *bhakti* because he has not committed any offence, spoken any blasphemy or engaged in any violence towards other living entities. In this way Bhagavān is supremely merciful. But if someone is behaving unfavourably towards others, then in hundreds of thousands of births he will not get *bhakti*.

Therefore, according to one's own natural proclivity, he should do everything for the service of Bhagavān. Then He will be pleased, the spiritual master will be pleased, all Vaiṣṇavas will be pleased, and everything will be correct. Remember that it is not for our own pleasure that we are doing everything, but for the pleasure of our *gurudeva*; only then is it fully correct.

This subject is very important, and especially for a *sādhaka* it is necessary to hear. We may be eager to hear talks about *rasa* and *līlā*, but we may not be so eager to hear about this subject. These points are essential to know because they are at the very root of *sādhana-bhajana*. If disregarding them we commit *aparādha*, we will leave the path of *bhakti* and our lives will be useless. Instead, we can prepare our hearts for serving the deity, the Vaiṣṇavas and the spiritual master in the correct way, and thereby achieve success in our *sādhana*.

Chapter Twelve

Ultimately Prema Cannot Be Described

Whenever we hear *hari-kathā*, we should listen with our hearts, and be sure to keep it in our hearts. Otherwise, the ear will hear, but the ear will not tell the heart, and it shouldn't be like that. What is told to our ears should arrive in our hearts, and we should try to bring that into practice. Then we will get the result of hearing. If we are not able to hear *hari-kathā* properly and not able to keep it in our hearts, then the spiritual greed that should arise from hearing such talks will not arise within us in this or in any other birth.

Śrīla Bhaktisiddhānta Sarasvatī Prabhupāda said that this world is deficient. This body is also deficient; everything here is deficient. But whatever we are undergoing in this world now, and whatever deficiencies there are, our aim is not to make them go away. We should not try for that in life. They will remain now, and they will remain for millions of years. What is the true purpose of human life – that should be ascertained in this lifetime. What is the aim of life? What should we do? This human birth is very valuable, because with it we can meet Bhagavān. We should definitely try for this in this very lifetime, and our goal should be ascertained before we are forty years of age. Generally, we see that after the age of forty one's desire and ability to take a new course in life is diminished. We may try to apply our minds to something new and then after some time our determination may fade and not return. Although it is certainly possible to change direction in life after the age of forty – and many have done it – the risk is there that one will become 'set in his ways'. So whatever situation you are in now as youths, at a tender age, you should put into practice the ideals that will lead to the goal of human life. Then the final result may come within a relatively short time or a very long time; that is a separate consideration. But your present age is very valuable. Therefore certainly before the age of forty a person should make the decision to fulfil the aim of human life. Because after that the age of fifty comes, and then there is an even greater chance that it will be too late. At that time, we may hear everything, but still never muster the firm determination to do what should be done.

In the name Gopa-kumāra, what is the meaning of *kumāra*? He is at a very tender age, and he met his *guru* at that age. Even after millions of years, when he finally received such mercy that he met Bhagavān, he still remained as a *kumāra*. From the day of meeting his *guru* he slowly came to understand *siddhānta* and became determined. He never abandoned the chanting of his *gopāla-mantra*. Wherever he went he kept the same determination, and he never changed his aim. We should follow that example. If our aim remains correct, then Kṛṣṇa in the form of the spiritual master, in the form of a Vaiṣṇava, in the form of the *śikṣā-guru*, and in other forms also, will give us help in the midst of our progress and send others to help us as well. Who sent Nārada to Gopa-kumāra? He met Nārada in Vaikuṇṭha, and Bhagavān as the Supersoul helps devotees in this way so that they can attain the goal of life. One who instructs us on how to attain Bhagavān is *guru*. For this purpose Nārada is wandering throughout the world, and it is through such a devotee that Bhagavān can help us.

Bhagavān is like a father and *jagad-guru*. The initiating spiritual master (*dīkṣā-guru*) is also *jagad-guru* and like a father, but a father will not instruct his daughter on how to serve her husband. He will not tell her how she is to behave when alone with her husband. Her mother will also not say. Who will say? Her close friend will be able to tell her. The example is also there that Kṛṣṇacandra is the beloved son of Nanda Bābā, and Nanda Bābā's younger brother is Sunanda. Though living with both of them, Kṛṣṇa is more affectionate with Sunanda. In the scriptures it has been described that He associates more with Sunanda. Sunanda is somewhat older than Kṛṣṇa, but he is Nanda's youngest brother. Therefore he is Kṛṣṇa's dear friend and like His father also. He can fight and quarrel with Kṛṣṇa too, but when Kṛṣṇa wants His father to agree to something, He approaches Sunanda, and Sunanda makes Nanda Bābā agree to it. He is very intimate with Kṛṣṇa.

Similarly, like a father, Bhagavān Himself will give us less instruction, but He will give it. In another form He will give it in great detail by sending someone who is dear to Him and that person will tell us everything. In the form of the instructing spiritual master (*śikṣā-guru*), Bhagavān will tell one everything. Nārada, as the *śikṣā-guru* of Gopa-kumāra, will tell him things that Jayanta, Gopa-kumāra's *dīkṣā-guru*, would not tell him. Just as the greatness of the *dīkṣā-guru* has been described, in the same way the glories of the *śikṣā-guru* have also been described in *Śrī Caitanya-caritāmṛta* and other scriptures.

There is some separation, *vipralambha-bhāva*, in devotees' love. It is such a peculiar sentiment that only *premī*, or loving, devotees can know it. Others cannot understand it, and upon seeing it, they even become frightened. In Purī, Mahāprabhu jumped into the ocean thinking that it was the Yamunā. A fisherman, taking his net, climbed into his boat and went out onto the ocean. Mahāprabhu's body appeared as if He had not eaten for a long time, and in this weak and fragile condition He entered into the fisherman's net. When the fisherman was drawing in his net, he felt the heavy weight and joyfully thought, "Today I have caught a big fish." Bringing the net into the boat, he returned to the shore. There, when he looked closer, he became frightened and thought, "What is this? A corpse has come into my net!" Having touched Mahāprabhu's body, the fisherman felt that a ghost had possessed him. Becoming overwhelmed with fear, he left his net and everything there and ran away.

Nearby, Svarūpa Dāmodara, Rāya Rāmānanda, Nityānanda Prabhu, Advaita Ācārya and all the devotees were searching for Mahāprabhu. They saw a madman on the shore of the ocean who was laughing, crying and calling out, "Hari! Hari!"

Svarūpa Dāmodara said to him, "What happened?"

The fisherman said, "A ghost has possessed me!"

Recognising the man's symptoms, Svarūpa Dāmodara said, "I know how to rid you of this ghost; I know the *mantra*." He slapped the fisherman a few times, recited a *mantra*, and then the fisherman came to his senses a bit. Then he said, "My friend, can you show us where you have seen this ghost?"

"From a distance I will show you, but I will not go near there!"

"All right."

Going to the place, from a distance the fisherman showed them. There in the net was Mahāprabhu, His body rolled into a ball in the posture of a child before birth. His joints were all dislocated, and His whole body was slack and elongated. Then Svarūpa Dāmodara told the fisherman, "Okay, you can go now and this 'ghost' will no longer disturb you." Then the devotees took Mahāprabhu out of the net, laid Him on the shore, and cleaned off His body. Surrounding Him, they started performing *kīrtana*, and after a little while Mahāprabhu came to His senses.

Seeing Mahāprabhu's condition, that fisherman became terrified. Like this, if any ordinary man sees such an advanced state of *bhakti*, will he desire *bhakti*? But loving devotees will understand. They will think, "When, in my meditation, will I also be able to have such a *darśana* of Kṛṣṇa as Mahāprabhu was experiencing? When will I receive such an opportunity?"

A devotee has to go through this intense separation to reach Kṛṣṇa. It is like the unhappiness of this world multiplied millions of times, and a devotee will have to feel that many times. Still, he will not be able to express it in words. Bhagavān Himself is not able to express it. Whoever is experiencing it will be unable to express it in words. Nowhere in the scriptures are the symptoms of *premī* devotees described completely. In *Śrīmad-Bhāgavatam*, the symptoms of the *gopīs'* state of intoxication and mad, senseless speech have only been described in brief; more than that has not been described. It is not possible. But we should understand the unhappiness of Śrīmatī Rādhikā and the *gopīs* in separation from Kṛṣṇa to be the ultimate transformation of happiness, the very culmination of happiness.

For example, when it is very hot and a few drops of rain begin to fall, it is very pleasant. When the month of Kārttika is starting and it begins to cool off, we like that very much. So coolness is welcome, but too much cold is unpleasant, such as when it freezes overnight and ice forms. But although cold and heat are complete opposites, it is an astonishing thing that when one takes a piece of ice in his hand, it feels as if it is burning. This burning sensation is the ultimate transformation of cold.

Similarly, in the realm of *bhakti*, when *kṛṣṇa-prema* becomes intensified and one experiences *vipralambha*, it seems that at that time he is very unhappy, but that is not actually unhappiness. It is the pinnacle of happiness. No one can describe the symptoms of that condition. What were the sentiments of Śrīmatī Rādhikā that Caitanya Mahāprabhu felt when He was locked in the Gambhīrā and was rubbing His face against the wall? The sentiments that were experienced by Rādhikā, the *bhāva* experienced by Mahāprabhu – has all of this been described? No. Therefore this is called *sva-saṁvedya-daśā*: it can only be understood by directly experiencing it oneself. It is not possible for anyone to describe it.

We cannot tell anyone about what divine bliss, what *ānanda*, has come within us as a result of meeting Kṛṣṇa.

Therefore, Nārada told Gopa-kumāra, "My dear friend, this desire to meet Kṛṣṇa which has arisen inside you by the influence of your *mantra* – this is *sva-saṁvedya-daśā*. With mere words I cannot make you understand completely this matter that has disturbed you, but I will try to describe it a little. The nature of *prema* is like that. That desire for the *prema* of your internal identity (*svarūpa*) can never be fulfilled here. That *svarūpa* is in *sakhya-bhāva*, and beyond that, pure *viśrambha*, or intimate, *sakhya-bhāva*. This *viśrambha-sakhya-bhāva* cannot be found in any place from Siddhaloka to Sadāśivaloka to Vaikuṇṭha, Ayodhyā, Mathurā or Dvārakā. It is found only in Vraja."

Then Nārada glanced around; Lakṣmī-devī was nowhere near, and no other eternal associates of Nārāyaṇa were around, so no one was listening to this conversation. If someone with a particular sentiment hears the words of someone with a higher sentiment, they will say something like, "Oh, he is blaspheming our Lord!" Therefore not everyone should hear such talks. That is why Nārada checked to ensure that no servant or friend of Lakṣmī, or Garuḍa, or anyone else was nearby. Then, after looking, he began speaking again. "Inside you there is so much *bhakti*. You can easily have heavenly enjoyment or liberation. You can even have the *prema* of Vaikuṇṭha, but the love for Śrī Rādhā and Kṛṣṇa that you are seeking is so difficult to obtain, so rare. By performing the appropriate sacrifice, you can attain residence in the heavenly planets, liberation, or even Vaikuṇṭha. By following the path of *jñāna* you can achieve liberation, and by way of *karma-yoga* you can go to heaven. But the *bhakti* that you desire cannot so easily be attained, even by millions of efforts. You will never obtain it by your own endeavour, so how will you receive it? Only if you unconditionally surrender to Śrī Rādhā-Kṛṣṇa and beg mercy from Them – then it may be possible. Our 'effort' is to pray for it. Our only prayer is that we can somehow offer Them our very soul. But trying to obtain this *prema* by our own effort? It is not possible. What you desire is very rare. It is obtainable – not that you can't get it, you can obtain it – but it is very difficult."

kadācid eva kasmaicit
tad-ekārtha-spṛhāvate
taṁ dadyād bhagavān bhaktiṁ
loka-bāhyāya dhīmate

Bṛhad-bhāgavatāmṛta (2.4.233)

If someone desires the *prema* of Vraja, then only if real spiritual greed has somehow or other arisen within them will they be able to obtain it. Without this greed it will never be possible. When a person really wants something, then by bribery, by thievery, by trickery, by fighting – by any means they will try to get it, and this greed is the root cause of *prema-bhakti*. Such transcendental greed is possible only when Bhagavān and His *premī, rasika* devotees are merciful to us. Kṛṣṇa will give the highest treasure only to those who have some special hankering for it and not to those who don't have this qualification.

What shape will this hankering take? "I want to serve Kṛṣṇa just as Subala does, or just as Madhumaṅgala, Śrīdāmā and others do." Is it possible that there is any special difference between the service of Śrīdāmā and the service of Subala? A very big difference is possible. Śrīdāmā has great love for Kṛṣṇa; as much as Subala or even more. But there is one hidden consideration here: Śrīdāmā is the brother of Śrīmatī Rādhikā. Therefore Kṛṣṇa is not always able to have free dealings with Śrīdāmā, because through him Rādhikā may come to know of something that Kṛṣṇa doesn't want Her to know about. But with Subala, Kṛṣṇa can speak openly and freely and completely reveal His heart. Therefore there is no distance between Kṛṣṇa and Subala. In this way there are differences between *sakhās*, and Gopa-kumāra's hankering is like that of Subala. He desires to serve Kṛṣṇa just as Subala does, remaining near to Him and taking the cows out to graze.

Suppose Kṛṣṇa is distributing *cintāmaṇi*, touchstone. Who is He distributing it to? To those who are qualified to receive it. And if someone else comes who is not qualified to receive *cintāmaṇi*, what will Kṛṣṇa give to him? He will give him some other stone that may shine more than *cintāmaṇi*, but which is not *cintāmaṇi*. He will give the greatest thing only to those who have some special greed for it, and for this reason, He sent Nārada to Gopa-kumāra, saying, "Increase his greed." But merely being greedy for a short time will not do. This greed is like a creeper: you must water it and protect it, and then it can grow all the way up to Vṛndāvana.

How does Kṛṣṇa increase someone's greed? Once Nārada was chanting his *mantra*. After chanting more and more, he attained *svarūpa-siddhi*. A very beautiful form with four arms appeared before him, and then at once disappeared. Now how much had his greed increased? Nārada started lamenting and crying until a voice from the sky said to him, "While residing within a material body you will not be able to have My direct company. For now you will remain in *svarūpa-siddhi* and you will not change your form. Then in your next birth, after giving up this form, you will attain *vastu-siddhi* and reside with Me eternally."

Therefore in sequence – first as the initiating spiritual master, then as the instructing spiritual master, then Bhagavān Himself comes as *guru* to increase our greed. So far the greed of Gopa-kumāra has reached up to Vaikuṇṭha, but now Nārada has come to increase his greed still further. As it increases more and more, finally Kṛṣṇa will give him the highest treasure, which is only given to someone who is fully greedy for it.

Prema-bhakti becomes mature in a similar way as a mango becomes ripe. There are many kinds of mango. Some mangos are so sweet, fragrant and delicious that upon tasting one of them, you won't want to stop eating until it is finished. Again and again you will keep putting the mango to your mouth, and as long as there is a little juice remaining in it, you will not discard it. So where is *prema* found in its full maturity? In the company of the Vrajavāsīs. In the company of the *nitya-siddha* associates of Kṛṣṇa it will be fully mature, and nowhere else. So at that time in Vaikuṇṭha, Gopa-kumāra's *prema* had not yet fully matured; it was still a little unripe.

Nārada is saying that there is no one capable of describing the nature of fully matured *prema*. Why? Because even Śrīmatī Rādhikā is not capable of it. In fact, if there is any person who is the most incapable of describing it, it is Rādhikā, because She Herself is fully immersed in that *rasa*. She will not be able to describe what She is experiencing, but those who remain aloof will be able to describe a little something of it. When a man has entered into *rasa*, what will he himself speak about it? He will not say anything. In any description of the state of Mahāprabhu's *prema*, we don't find in any place that He Himself described it. In some places Svarūpa Dāmodara has described it in poetry, Rūpa Gosvāmī described a little of it, and by hearing from Rūpa and Raghunātha, Kṛṣṇadāsa Kavirāja Gosvāmī described something of it, but he was unable to describe it completely.

Nārada is saying, "In describing this *prema*, what will I say? I am capable of saying something about the symptoms of it, but most people will misunderstand and take another meaning. I may say, 'Oh, Rādhikā is dying in separation and crying in pain, the poor girl has become senseless! For a long time Rādhikā remained senseless. The tears from Her eyes made Her clothing wet, and She rubbed the dust of Kṛṣṇa's feet on Her shawl and the rest of Her clothes. With the tears related to Kṛṣṇa and the dust related to Kṛṣṇa combined, Rādhikā's clothes became unclean, but She refused to change them. She was firmly determined that She would wear no other clothes except those that were saturated with

Her tears for Kṛṣṇa and His foot-dust.' But upon hearing this, most people will say, 'Oh, such suffering!'"

When Uddhava went to Vṛndāvana to deliver a message from Kṛṣṇa and first saw the condition of the Vrajavāsīs, he said, "I have heard that their love for Kṛṣṇa is very deep, but for so long they have been in so much agony! Mother Yaśodā is dying!" But will Rādhikā, Nanda Bābā or Mother Yaśodā ever leave Vṛndāvana? Will any *gopī* ever leave? Will even any of the young servants of the *gopīs* leave? No. They are experiencing a kind of ecstasy that even Uddhava could not fully understand. Therefore, even the servants who sweep Rādhikā's home are considered to be on a higher level than Uddhava. Uddhava cannot attain that high kind of sentiment. The *gopīs* are all crying, and their servants are trying to console them, but still none of them will ever leave there. In the end Uddhava left Vṛndāvana unable to fully comprehend that high sentiment.

The symptoms of *prema* in its mature state are not a thing that can be spoken of, so how can it be written about in the scriptures? And if they were written, then what would be the result? In *Śrīmad-Bhāgavatam* only a little has been described about the meeting of Śrī Rādhā and Kṛṣṇa, and many people say that there is some detestable, sinful activity described in the *Bhāgavatam*. Many people have said this. How will all of these people understand the *Bhāgavatam*? Only a little has been told, and they say that it is filthy. So if even more of it were described, then what would happen? Yet if the *Bhāgavatam* were not there, the devotees would not be able to maintain their lives because the *Bhāgavatam* is most dear to them. If you give a piece of ginger to a monkey, what will he do? He will look at it, and then merely discard it. Monkeys do not know that ginger is valuable for digestion and health. So these high sentiments from the *Bhāgavatam* should not be described to ignorant people. They are not spoken even to Rukmiṇī or Satyabhāmā, so what to speak of others?

But there is one more point here: those who are *rasika*, who are *sva-saṁvedya-daśā*, who have experienced *prema* themselves – they will not describe it, but they will recognise it when they see it. Besides Svarūpa Dāmodara, no one else could understand the *bhāva* of Caitanya Mahāprabhu. He understood it, but never spoke of it. There is a verse that Mahāprabhu was calling out with a faltering voice before Jagannātha's cart:

yaḥ kaumāra-haraḥ sa eva hi varas tā eva caitra-kṣapās
te conmīlita-mālatī-surabhayaḥ prauḍhāḥ kadambānilāḥ
sā caivāsmi tathāpi tatra surata-vyāpāra-līlā-vidhau
revā-rodhasi vetasī-taru-tale cetaḥ samutkaṇṭhate

Padyāvalī (382)

That same lover who stole away My heart during My youth is now again My master. These are the same moonlit nights in the month of Caitra, and the same breezes from the *kadamba* forest are blowing the same fragrance from the *mālatī* flowers. I am also the same lover as before, but My heart is not satisfied here. I desire to return with Him to the bank of the river Revā, under the *vetasī* tree.

When Mahāprabhu spoke that verse, only Svarūpa Dāmodara understood, but then it became apparent that Rūpa Gosvāmī also understood. Perceiving the sentiment within Mahāprabhu's heart, Rūpa Gosvāmī composed a parallel verse. He wrote it on a palm leaf and placed it in the thatched roof of his hut before going to bathe:

priyaḥ so 'yaṁ kṛṣṇaḥ sahacari kuru-kṣetra-militas
tathāhaṁ sā rādhā tad idam ubhayoḥ saṅgama-sukham
tathāpy antaḥ-khelan-madhura-muralī-pañcama-juṣe
mano me kālindī-pulina-vipināya spṛhayati

Padyāvalī (383)

My dear friend, I have now again met My lover, Śrī Kṛṣṇa, here at Kurukṣetra. I am the same Rādhā, and We are experiencing the happiness of meeting. Still, I desire for Us to return to the bank

> of the Yamunā beneath the trees of the forest there, where I can hear Him playing the sweet melody of the fifth note on the flute.

Mahāprabhu and Svarūpa Dāmodara thought that only they could understand this sentiment, but upon seeing this poem of Rūpa Gosvāmī, they could see that Rūpa Gosvāmī also understood. This is *sva-saṁvedya-daśā.*

Therefore Nārada told Gopa-kumāra, "You are an eternal resident of Vraja, not of this Vaikuṇṭha. Now the mango is ripening; a little fragrance is coming from it. In a few days the mango will be fully mature, and its taster will see that it has ripened, its fragrance has come, and now juice will come out of it. So taking it, he will relish it. Such a day is coming. Now the time is very near when you will go to Vraja and all of your desires will be fulfilled."

Glossary

A

ābhāsa – the semblance of something.

abhiṣeka – bathing of a deity in milk, yoghurt, water and other ingredients.

ācārya – spiritual preceptor; one who teaches by example.

ānanda – divine bliss or ecstasy.

anarthas – unwanted desires in the heart, which impede one's advancement in devotional life.

anurāga – an intensified stage of *prema*; a stage in the development from *prema* up to *mahābhāva*. In *Ujjvala-nīlamaṇi* (14.146) *anurāga* has been defined as follows: "Although one regularly meets with the beloved and is well acquainted with the beloved, the ever-fresh sentiment of intense attachment causes the beloved to be newly experienced at every moment as if one has never before had any experience of that person. The attachment that inspires such a feeling is known as *anurāga*."

aparādha – an offence committed against the holy name, the Vaiṣṇavas, the spiritual master, the scriptures, holy places or the deity.

ārati – the ceremony of offering a deity articles of worship, such as incense, lamp, flowers and fan, accompanied by bell-ringing and chanting.

arcana – deity worship; one of the nine primary processes of devotional service.

āsakti – attachment; this especially refers to attachment to the Lord and His eternal associates.

ātmā – the soul.

avatāra – an incarnation; one who descends.

B

bhagavad-bhakti – see *bhakti.*

Bhagavān – the Supreme Lord, Śrī Kṛṣṇa.

bhajana – spiritual practices, especially hearing, chanting and meditating upon the holy names, form, qualities and pastimes of Śrī Kṛṣṇa.

bhakti – the word *bhakti* comes from the root *bhaj*, which means 'to serve'. Therefore the primary meaning of the word *bhakti* is to render service. The performance of activities meant exclusively for the pleasure of Śrī Kṛṣṇa, which are done in a favourable spirit saturated with love, which are devoid of all other desires and which are not covered by the pursuits of fruitive activity (*karma*) or the cultivation of knowledge aimed at merging one's existence into that of the Lord (*jñāna*), is called *bhakti.*

bhāva – (1) spiritual emotions, love or sentiments; (2) the initial stage of perfection in devotion (*bhāva-bhakti*).

bhoga – foodstuffs that are to offered to the deity.

brahmacārī – a member of the first *āśrama* (stage of life) in the *varṇāśrama* system; a celibate, unmarried student.

brahma – the impersonal, all-pervading feature of the Lord, which is devoid of attributes and qualities.

brāhmaṇa – the intellectual class amongst the four castes within the Vedic social system.

brahmāṇḍa – an egg-shaped material universe.

C

caitya-guru – the Supersoul situated within the heart, who gives spiritual instruction and guidance.

cāmara – a fan made of the hair of a yak's tail, employed especially as part of the paraphernalia offered to the deity.

campā – the fragrant yellowish-white flower of the Michelia *campaka* tree.

caraṇāmṛta – nectar from the feet of the Lord. Substances such as milk, honey, yoghurt, clarified butter and rose water are used to bathe the feet of the deity. The nectar that is collected from that is known as *caraṇāmṛta.*

D

dāsya – one of the five primary relationships with the Lord that is established in the heart when one is in the stage of *bhāva* or *prema*; love for or attraction to the Lord that is expressed in the mood of a servant.

dhāma – a holy place of pilgrimage; the abode of Śrī Bhagavān, where He appears and enacts His transcendental pastimes.

dharma – religion in general; the socio-religious duties prescribed in the scriptures for different classes of persons in the *varṇāśrama* system.

G

ghee – clarified butter.

gopas – the cowherd boys who serve Kṛṣṇa in the mood of intimate friends. This may also refer to the elderly *gopas* who serve Kṛṣṇa in the mood of parental affection.

gopīs – the young cowherd maidens of Vraja, headed by Śrīmatī Rādhikā, who serve Śrī Kṛṣṇa in the mood of amorous love. This may also refer to the elderly *gopīs*, headed by Mother Yaśodā, who serve Kṛṣṇa in the mood of parental affection.

gosvāmī – one who is the master of his senses, a title for those in the renounced order of life. This often refers to the renowned followers of Caitanya Mahāprabhu who adopted the lifestyle of mendicants.

gṛhastha – one who is in household life; the second stage of life (*āśrama*) within the Vedic social system (*varṇāśrama*).

guru-paramparā – the disciplic succession through which spiritual knowledge is transmitted by bona fide spiritual masters.

H

harināma – the holy name of the Lord, especially referring to the *mahā-mantra*.

hlādinī – this refers to the Lord's internal potency (*svarūpa-śakti*) that is predominated by *hlādinī*. *Hlādinī* is the potency that relates to the *ānanda*, or bliss, aspect of the Supreme Lord. Although the Supreme Lord is the embodiment of all pleasure, *hlādinī* is that potency by which He relishes transcendental bliss and causes others to taste bliss.

I

ī´vara – the Supreme God of all gods.

J

jagad-guru – one who is qualified to act as a spiritual master for anyone in the entire world.

japa – very soft utterance or whispering of the holy names of the Lord to oneself; usually refers to the practice of chanting *harināma* on *tulasī* beads.

jīva – the eternal, individual living entity, who in the conditioned state of material existence assumes a material body in any of the innumerable species of life.

jñāna – (1) knowledge in general; (2) knowledge leading to impersonal liberation.

K

kalpa – the period of time equivalent to one day in the life of Lord Brahmā.

kāma-gāyatrī – a confidential *mantra* received from the spiritual master at the time of second initiation.

karatālas – hand cymbals used in congregational glorification of the Lord.

karma-kāṇḍa – a division of the Vedas that relates to the performance of ceremonial acts and sacrificial rites directed towards either material benefit or liberation.

kīrtana – congregational singing of the Lord's holy names, which is sometimes accompanied by music. This may also refer to loud individual chanting of the holy name as well as oral descriptions of the Lord's names, form, qualities, associates and pastimes. *Kīrtana* is one of the nine most important limbs of devotion.

ki´ora – an adolescent boy.

ki´orī – an adolescent girl.

kuñja – a grove or bower; a natural shady retreat, the sides and roof of which are formed mainly by trees and climbing plants.

kuṅkuma – a powder used by women for personal decoration.

L

līlā – the divine and astonishing pastimes of Śrī Bhagavān and His eternal associates, which grant all auspiciousness for the living entity, which have no connection with this mundane world and which lie beyond the grasp of the material senses and mind.

līlā-avatāra – an incarnation of the Supreme Lord that appears solely for the purpose of performing pastimes.

M

mādhurya-rasa – one of the five primary relationships with Kṛṣṇa established in the stage of *bhāva* and *prema*; love or attachment towards Kṛṣṇa that is expressed in the mood of a lover. This mood is eternally present in the *gopīs* of Vraja.

māna – an intensified stage of *prema*; a stage in the development from *prema* up to *mahābhāva*. It is described in *Ujjvala-nīlamaṇi* (14.96): "When *sneha* reaches exultation, thus causing one to experience the sweetness of the beloved in ever-new varieties, yet externally takes on a crooked feature, it is known as *māna*."

mañjarī – a young maidservant of Śrīmatī Rādhikā.
mandira – a temple.
manvantara – the lifespan of one Manu; that is, seventy-one *yugas*, each *yuga* being 4,320,000 years in duration.
mahābhāva – the highest stage of *prema*, divine love. In *Ujjvala-nīlamaṇi* (14.154) *mahābhāva* is defined thus: "When *anurāga* reaches a special state of intensity, it is known as *bhāva* or *mahābhāva*. This stage of intensity has three characteristics: (i) *anurāga* reaches the state of *sva-saṁvedya*, which means that it becomes the object of its own experience; (ii) it becomes *prakāśita*, radiantly manifest, which means that all eight *sāttvika-bhāvas* become prominently displayed; and (iii) it attains the state of *yāvad-āśraya-vṛtti*, which means that the active ingredient of the intensified state of *anurāga* transmits the experience of Rādhā and Kṛṣṇa's *bhāva* to whomever may be present and qualified to receive it."
mantra – a spiritual sound vibration that delivers the mind from its material conditioning and illusion when repeated over and over; a Vedic hymn, prayer or chant.
māyāvādī – one who advocates the doctrine of impersonalism.
mṛdaṅga – a clay drum used in congregational glorification of the Lord.
mūrti – a form of the Lord, usually referring to the deity form.

N

niṣṭhā – firm faith; established devotional practice that does not waver at any time.
nitya-siddha – eternally perfected devotees.

P

parikramā – circumambulation of holy places.
praṇaya – an intensified stage of *prema*; a stage in the development from *prema* up to *mahābhāva*. It is described in *Ujjvala-nīlamaṇi*

(14.108): "When *māna* assumes a feature of unrestrained intimacy known as *viśrambha*, learned authorities refer to it as *praṇaya*." The word *viśrambha* used in this verse means 'complete confidence devoid of any restraint or formality'. This confidence causes one to consider one's life, mind, intelligence, body and possessions to be one in all respects with the life, mind, intelligence and body of the beloved.

prasāda – literally meaning mercy, especially refers to the remnants of food offered to the deity.

pūjā – offering of worship.

pujārī – a priest who formally offers *pūjā*, worship, to the deity form of the Lord.

puruṣa-avatāra – one of the three Viṣṇu incarnations involved in the creation, maintenance and annihilation of this world: Kāraṇodakaśāyī Viṣṇu, Garbhodakaśāyī Viṣṇu and Kṣīrodakaśāyī Viṣṇu.

R

rāga – (1) a deep attachment that is permeated by spontaneous and intense absorption in the object of one's affection. The primary characteristic of *rāga* is a deep and overpowering thirst for the object of one's affection. The desire for water is called thirst. When the body is deprived of water this thirst arises. The greater the thirst the greater the longing for water. When this thirst reaches the point that without water, one can no longer maintain the body, it is known as an overpowering thirst. Similarly, when the loving thirst to please the object of one's affection becomes so intense that in the absence of such service one is on the verge of giving up his life, it is known as *rāga*. This *rāga* is the basis of the *rāgātmikā* devotees' *bhakti*; (2) an intensified stage of *prema*; a stage in the development from *prema* up to *mahābhāva*. It is described as follows in *Ujjvala-nīlamaṇi* (14.126): "When *praṇaya* reaches exultation, thus causing even extreme misery to be experienced within the heart as happiness, it is known as *rāga*." In Jīva Gosvāmī's commentary on this verse, he explains that if by accepting some misery there is a chance of meeting with Kṛṣṇa, then that misery becomes a source of great happiness. And where happiness affords one no opportunity to meet with Kṛṣṇa, that happiness becomes the source of great distress. When such a state is experienced, it is known as *rāga*.

rāgānugā-bhakti – an elevated stage of devotion that is motivated by spontaneous attraction or love.

rasa – the spiritual transformation of the heart that takes place when the perfected state of love for Kṛṣṇa, known as *rati*, is converted into 'liquid' emotions by combination with various types of transcendental ecstasy.

roṭī – Indian-style unleavened bread that is oven-baked.

ruci – taste; the fifth stage in the development of the creeper of devotion.

S

sabjī – cooked vegetables

sac-cid-ānanda – that which is eternal, composed of spiritual consciousness and full of transcendental bliss.

sad-guru – a perfected spiritual master.

sādhaka – one who follows a spiritual discipline with the objective of achieving pure devotion for Śrī Kṛṣṇa.

sādhana – the stage of devotional life in which a spiritual discipline is performed for the purpose of bringing about the manifestation of ecstatic, pure love for Śrī Kṛṣṇa (*bhāva*).

sādhana-siddha – devotees who have attained perfection through spiritual practice.

sādhu – a saintly person.

sakhā – a male friend, companion or attendant.

sakhī – a female friend, companion or attendant.

sakhya – one of the five primary relationships with Kṛṣṇa that is established in the heart when one is in the stage of *bhāva* or *prema*; love or attachment for the Lord that is expressed in the mood of a friend.

´ālagrāma-´ilā – self-manifesting deities of Nārāyaṇa in the form of small, round black stones that are found in the Gandakī River in the Himālayas.

sampradāya – a school of religious thought.

saṁbandha-jñāna – knowledge regarding *sambandha-tattva*, the mutual relationship between the Lord, the living entities and the material energy. The word *sambandha* means connection, relationship or binding. The living entities are eternally and inseparably connected to the Supreme Lord. Therefore He is the true object of relationship. The general relationship between the living entities and the Supreme Lord is one of servant and served. However, in the perfected stage of devotion one becomes established in a specific relationship with the Lord either as a servant, friend, parent or lover.

saṁvit – this refers to the internal potency (*svarūpa-śakti*) that is predominated by *saṁvit*. It is the potency that relates to *cit*, the cognisant aspect of the Supreme Lord. Although the Supreme Lord is the embodiment of knowledge, *saṁvit* is the potency by which He knows Himself and causes others to know Him.

saṅkīrtana – loud congregational chanting of the Lord's holy names.

sannyāsa – renounced ascetic life; the fourth stage of life (*āśrama*) within the Vedic social system (*varṇāśrama*).

sannyāsī – one in the renounced order of life.

sevā – service, attendance on, reverence, devotion to.

siddhānta – philosophical doctrine or precept; demonstrated conclusion; established end; admitted truth.

sneha – an intensified stage of *prema*; a stage in the development from *prema* up to *mahābhāva*. It is described in *Ujjvala-nīlamaṇi*

(14.79): "When *prema* ascends to its ultimate limit, intensifies one's perception of the object of love, and melts the heart, it is known as *sneha*."

´raddhā – faith. This refers to faith in the statements of the scriptures that is awakened after accumulating pious merit through the performance of devotional activities over many births.

´rī vigraha – the deity form of the Lord.

svarūpa-´akti – the Lord's internal potency.

svayaṁvara – the ancient Vedic marriage ceremony.

T

tattva – truth, reality, philosophical principle; the essence or substance of anything.

tilaka – clay markings worn on the forehead and other parts of the body by Vaiṣṇavas, signifying their devotion to Śrī Kṛṣṇa or Viṣṇu, and consecrating the body as the Lord's temple.

tulasī – a sacred plant whose leaves and blossoms are used by Vaiṣṇavas in the worship of Śrī Kṛṣṇa; the wood is also used for chanting beads and neck beads.

V

vaidhī-bhakti – devotion that is prompted by the rules and regulations of the scriptures.

vaijayantī – a garland made of five varieties of flower and which reaches the knees.

vānaprastha – a member of the third stage of life (*āśrama*) in the Vedic social system; retired life that entails freedom from family responsibilities and the acceptance of spiritual vows.

vandana – the offering of prayers.

varṇā´rama-dharma – the Vedic social system, which organises society into four occupational divisions (*varṇas*) and four stages of life (*āśramas*).

vātsalya – one of the five primary relationships with Kṛṣṇa that is established in the heart when one is in the stage of *bhāva* or *prema*; love or attachment for the Lord expressed in the mood of a parent.

Y

yoga-nidrā – mystic slumber induced by the Lord's Yogamāyā potency.

yuga – one of the four ages described in the Vedas: Satya-yuga, Tretā-yuga, Dvāpara-yuga and Kali-yuga. The duration of each *yuga* is said to be, respectively: 1,728,000; 1,296,000; 864,000; and 432,000 years. The descending numbers represent a corresponding physical and moral deterioration of mankind in each age.

Verse Index

H

I

J

K

M

N

T

V

Y

Worldwide Centers & Contacts

Please contact us at the address stamped or written on the first page of this book, or at the listings below:

INDIA

- **Mathura** - Sri Kesavaji Gaudiya Matha
  Jawahar Hata, U.P. 281001 (Opp. Dist. Hospital)
  Tel: 0565 250-2334, e-mail: mathuramath@gmail.com
- **New Delhi** - Sri Ramana-vihari Gaudiya Matha
  Block B-3, Janakpuri, New Delhi 110058
  (Near musical fountain park) Tel: 011 25533568, 9810192540
- **New Delhi** - Karol Bagh Center - Rohini-nandana
  9A/39 Channa Market, WEA, Karol Bagh
  Tel.: 9810398406, 9810636370, Email: purebhakti.kb@gmail.com
- **Vrindavan** - Sri Rupa-Sanatana Gaudiya Matha
  Dan Gali, U.P. Tel: 0565 244-3270
- **Vrindavan** - Gopinath Bhavan
  Ranapat Ghat, Seva Kunja, Vrindavan 281121, U.P.
  Tel: 0565 244-3359, e-mail: vasantidasi@gmail.com
- **Jagannath Puri** - Jayasri Damodar Gaudiya Math
  Chakratirtha. Tel: 06752-229695
- **Bangalore** - Sri Madana Mohan Gaudiya Matha
  245/1 29th Cross, Kaggadasa pura,Balaji layout, Bangalore-93
  Tel: 08904427754 e-mail: giridharidas@gmail.com

USA

- **Gaudiya Vedanta Publications Offices**
  Tel: (800) 681-3040 ext. 108, e-mail: orders@bhaktiprojects.org
- **Houston** - Preaching Center
  Tel: (1) 713-984 8334, e-mail: byshouston@gmail.com
- **Los Angeles** – Sri Sri Radha Govinda Temple
  305 Rose Avenue, Venice, California 90291
  Tel: (1) 310-310 2817

UNITED KINGDOM & IRELAND

- **Birmingham** - International Distributor
  Tel: (44) 153648-1769, e-mail: jivapavana@googlemail.com
- **London** - Ganga-mata Gaudiya Matha
  Email: gangamatajis@yahoo.co.uk
- **Galway** - Family Center,
  Tel: 353 85-1548200, e-mail: loveisgod108@hotmail.com

GUYANA

- **East Cost Demerara**- Sri Sri Radha Govinda Gaudiya Matha
  156 Area A Bladen Hall School Road
  Tel: 0592 270-4102, 0592 233-2898
  e-mail: radhagovindagy@yahoo.com